GALATIANS

UNITING DIVIDED PEOPLE

THE TRUTH OF THE GOSPEL

HENRY HON

www.onebody.life

PREFACE

I have studied Paul's epistle to the Galatians for almost 50 years, but I have never seen his heart and motivation for writing this letter. Now that I do, his words have come alive as never before. It feels as though I discovered a new book in the Bible.

The catalyst that opened my eyes occurred when I realized the event that precipitated Paul to write this epistle. Paul wrote Galatians in response to Peter and Jewish followers of Jesus when they divided from Gentile believers at Antioch. It was the only time since Christ's resurrection that one of the original apostles was publicly rebuked. In his rebuke Paul declared Peter's dividing from these Gentile believers in Jesus was "against the truth of the gospel" (Gal. 2:5, 14).

Paul used this event to preach the truth of the gospel and expose the distortion of the gospel which had divided believers since the resurrection of Christ. The popular doctrines gleaned from Galatians relating to righteousness and holiness risk becoming distorted, even perverted, if not viewed in light of Paul's goal of uniting divided people in Christ.

Therefore, Galatians is extremely relevant today for God's increasingly fractured and divided people. *Galatians: Uniting Divided People* unpacks how Paul exposes the source of divisions and the solution for uniting into one diverse believers in the Body of Christ: His *ekklesia*.

Henry Hon
Author

To Bill Polsley

Grace & peace!

TABLE OF CONTENTS

1

A DISTORTED GOSPEL: SUBTLY DESTROYING THE EKKLESIA

Paul's epistle to the Galatians created a foundational understanding of key Christian doctrines throughout the last five centuries. Justification by faith versus works of the law, the crucified and the inner life ("Christ lives in me") were significant themes discovered in Galatians. Evangelists worldwide have used this book to promote being made right with God through the redemption by the blood of Jesus Christ on the cross as the primary result of the gospel of Jesus Christ. Others have used Galatians to apply the crucified and inner life to a believer's journey in holiness and discipleship.

The underpinning Scriptures for this beautiful truth of justification by faith are the following verses:

> yet we know that a person is not justified by works of the law, but through faith in Jesus Christ, so we also have believed in Christ Jesus, in order to be justified by faith in Christ and not by works of the law, because by works of the law no one will be justified[1].
>
> –Gal 2:16

> … "The righteous (just) shall live by faith."
>
> –Gal. 3:11

There are other verses in Galatians which highlight that working to keep God's law can never justify people, but only through faith in Jesus Christ can a person be justified (made righteous) before God.

---

1   Unless otherwise noted, all quotation of Scriptures is from English Standard Version (ESV)

Additionally, many crucial verses unveil a life for Christians who desire to live a life of Christ in holiness beyond justification. This may be the most prominent:

> I have been crucified with Christ. It is no longer I who live, but Christ who lives in me. And the life I now live in the flesh I live by faith in the Son of God, who loved me and gave himself for me.
> —Gal 2:20

Based on this verse and subsequent portions supporting this, serious Christians have taught the following matters: the crucified life and Christ as the believer's inner life. Sincere seekers have resolved to live a life of self-denial wherein they are "crucified with Christ" and to learn Christ living in them for victory — the "overcoming Life."

The healthy teachings relating to personal justification and living a life of sanctification to have the fruit of the Spirit; thereby, becoming a follower or disciple of Christ, has been taught by many Bible teachers, great and small.

The purpose of this book is not to rehash or bring new light to these topics of justification and sanctification in one's Christian journey.

Some may consider they are not affected by, nor are they drawn to the Mosaic laws or Jewish traditions. Therefore, they would claim this letter does not apply to them. These might say Galatians is not needed for their present learning and experience if one has already concluded that the practice of circumcision as a religious ritual or following the Mosaic law is no longer necessary for either salvation or sanctification.

Here is what may be explosive and new: this book brings forth the nexus of the letter to the Galatians. **The purpose and goal of both justification and sanctification is the practical oneness in the Body of Christ.** This is the heart of the gospel Paul declared (Gal. 1:8-9). Paul wrote this letter specifically to bring divided and contrary believers together into one. He calls these believers in unity: Abraham's seed (Gal. 3:27-29) is the New Creation wherein "peace and mercy" are afforded — they are the Israel of God (Gal. 6:15-16).

According to Galatians, Christians who have gone back to the works of the law have been deceived by a perversion of the gospel (i.e., a distorted, perverted, different, or another gospel). As a result of such works of the flesh, they became divided from other believers with differing perspectives, especially between Jewish and Gentile believers. Whereas the evidence and result of one justified by faith and living a crucified life in the Spirit is the ability to love and continue in fellowship with those dissimilar to themselves. This is the truth of the gospel!

Contemporary Christians increasingly divide into more and more factions. This new insight makes Galatians relevant considering these rampant divisions among believers today — let alone the racial and socio-economic tensions afflicting the West and throughout the world. These divisions cause the world to mock the followers of Christ, Satan to continue his domain on earth, believers to lose their blessings (inheritance) in Christ, and God still waiting for the expression of His glory from His people.

Galatians then is Paul's defense of the gospel of Jesus Christ, showing the reality behind what the gospel has accomplished: the oneness of the Body of Christ. Ironically, the traditional, singular focus of righteousness and holiness has often caused divisions in the Body of Christ.

Historical Background

The gospel, after the death and resurrection of Jesus Christ, was first preached to the Jews during the day of Pentecost in Jerusalem (Acts 1-2). The powerful effect of this initial outburst of the gospel was that thousands came to Christ and into the Lord's ekklesia (mistranslated to "church") which came into existence in fulfillment of what Jesus said He would build in Matthew 16:17-19. Although there was a diversity of people from all over the world, they were all Jews or converts to Judaism — if not genetically, then religiously. They accepted the law of Moses and were in Jerusalem for the Jewish feast of Weeks (aka Pentecost) according to the Hebrew Scriptures.

However, the Lord's calling and salvation were not just for Jews but also the Gentile nations (Gk. "*ethnos*" or "ethnic people groups"). God desires all men to be saved and come to the knowledge of the truth (1 Tim. 2:4). Therefore, His kingdom includes people from every tribe, language, people, and nation (Rev. 5:9-10). Nevertheless, the Jews in those days, although many became followers of Jesus Christ, still considered themselves to be God's uniquely chosen people with an allegiance to the law of Moses (Acts 21:20) and the "separation" from the nations in accordance with various laws or ordinances derived from the Torah.

However, at the house of Cornelius, God did something amazing and incredible from a first-century Jewish perspective (Acts 10:45). Gentiles — those being "called out from the nations" — received and believed the gospel of Jesus Christ. Indeed, the Holy Spirit fell on them just as He had upon the Jews. The Jewish believers deemed they were unique in receiving the Spirit. They were exclusively the people of God, and the Almighty was opening their eyes to the Messiah and the subsequent salvation offered through Him: the Lord Jesus Christ. Nevertheless, God's eternal purpose included not only the Jews but also people from all nations — even those outside the immediate covenant according to the law of Moses.

Jewish believers associated with circumcision were "astonished that the gift of the Holy Spirit had been poured out even on Gentiles" (Acts 10:22-48). This distinction was not necessarily between Jews and Gentiles, but rather between the circumcised and the uncircumcised (Acts 11:2-3). We will come back to this critical point later in this book.

God in the New Covenant is no longer a respecter of persons: He no longer has a "chosen" ethnic race as in the First Covenant (Heb. 8:7). Instead, "whosoever will" from any tribe, language, people, or nation can believe into Jesus Christ, be saved, and be His people (Rom. 10:11-12). Although this is now the case, these Jewish believers of the circumcision did not have a complete revelation of the New Covenant. Therefore, although they became genuine followers of Jesus Christ, they considered themselves superior to those from other nations. Consequently, they were forceful in their efforts to convert Gentile Christians to Judaism, believing these recent converts to Jesus must now abide by the laws of Moses with "circumcision" being foremost in this "law keeping" (Acts 15:1-5).

Those of the circumcision, Jewish Christians (in the main), had a missionary zeal to convert Gentile Christians to abide by the Law of Moses and be circumcised. Wherever Paul went on his missionary journeys preaching the gospel of Jesus Christ, Jewish Christians from Jerusalem, in their zeal for the Law of Moses, followed him confusing Gentile believers concerning the "truth of the gospel." They would tell these Gentile believers they could not have full salvation unless they would abide by the requirements found in the laws of Moses and be circumcised (Gal. 2:12-14; 4:24-25). In Acts 15:5 it says, "Then some of the believers who belonged to the party of the Pharisees stood up and said, 'The Gentiles must be circumcised and required to keep the law of Moses'" (NIV).

There were several compelling reasons to listen to these Jewish believers. They were from Jerusalem, where Pentecost took place, the city of the twelve apostles, and where the half-brother of Jesus Himself (James) was the top leader. They went out to these Gentile believers as spies (Gal. 2:4), and were able to mingle easily with Gentile Christians. Yet, they had an agenda — a hidden motive: they wanted to convert these Gentile Christians to come under the law of Moses.

The apostle Paul preached the gospel of Jesus Christ to the Gentile world (Gal. 2:7-8). He cared for them as a spiritual mother and father for their growth and maturity (1 Thess. 2:7-11; 1 Cor. 4:15). However, compared to these born-again Jewish preachers, he seemed insignificant and weak (2 Cor. 10:10). Therefore, he defended himself for the sake of these Gentile believers so they would come back to Christ alone (Gal. 1:11-24; 2 Cor. 10-11).

Keeping Gentile believers from being distracted from salvation through faith alone in Christ was the underlying struggle in most of Paul's epistles. In Acts, Romans, and Galatians, this struggle was overtly fought. Behind this apparent conflict was a deeper purpose, which is God's eternal purpose based on His salvation but extended beyond the bounds of Judaism: ". . . but also for the scattered children of God, to bring them together and make them one" (John 11:52). The ultimate result of the New Covenant of grace through faith (versus law and works) is the Lord building up of His ekklesia (unfortunately, this word "ekklesia" has been mistranslated to the word "church," which means a physical "house of worship").

Ekklesia was the forum for democracy invented by the Greeks around 600 B.C.; it was their "democratic legislative assembly."[2] Jesus in Matthew 16:18 appropriated this forum and said that He would build His own ekklesia. While democracy (Gk., *ekklesia*) has become the dominant form of government worldwide, it also exposes intolerance, hatred, and divisions among diverse and contrary people racially, socially, and politically. In today's contentious environment, confusion and division within a democratic society seems to be increasing as manifested in the USA. Additionally, the Christian institutional system of churches is not helping. Instead, it has further divided Christians through various categorizing and groupings over biblical interpretations and practices.

---

2   My book "One Ekklesia" did an in depth study into the historical usage of "ekklesia" and how the Lord's ekklesia mirrored the Greek ekklesia

God will use this forum of democracy (*ekklesia*) to build His own "spiritual democracy" where the most diverse and contrary groups of people can come together and love one another. This love for one another manifests diversity in unity which is the prime testimony of the Trinity: three, distinctly Father, Son, and Holy Spirit, yet inseparably ONE. They are individually joined to the Lord Jesus, and through this union they love one another in unity — regardless of the background from which they hail. The Lord's ekklesia is a conglomeration of disparate people who are one in Him through faith in Jesus Christ.

The Scriptures call the Lord's ekklesia "lampstands" throughout the earth (Rev. 1:20). What a contrast between the world's democracies and the Lord's diverse people in unity! The Lord's ekklesia is the light radiating. People who normally would be enemies or in opposition to one another retain their convictions and differences and shine forth with love for one another. This can only exist through the work of redemption in Jesus Christ — His death and resurrection. Therefore, Jesus prayed for His diverse people to be one to cause the world to believe in His reality (John 17:21, 23).

This is the "truth of the gospel": breaking down religious barriers between Jewish believers and those called out from among the nations through faith alone in the finished work of Christ on the cross!

Galatians will become a new epistle to students of the Bible once they read it with Paul's original intention of solving divisions and separation within God's ekklesia, the Body of Christ. In fact, God's eternal purpose is predicated on the building up of His ekklesia, which will manifest His multifaceted wisdom to shame His enemies (Eph. 3:10-11). Justification and the inner life of holiness are important, but as procedures, these are secondary to the building up of His ekklesia. God's ekklesia has various descriptions throughout the New Testament, such as: Temple, Kingdom, Household, Bride, Body, New Man, Perfect Man, Commonwealth of Israel, the Israel of God, New Creation, and the New Jerusalem.

Generally, Bible teachers have lost sight of God's goal of His eternal purpose for His ekklesia. Instead, most teachers have focused on justification and sanctification. Concentrating on these two matters of one's personal salvation journey has contributed to divisions and conflicts among Christians.

An illustration: Our group plans to travel from the USA to Ibadan, Nigeria. The method for this trip is by airplane and bus. We discuss and debate the plane trip as to what kind of airplane, who the pilot is, how many stops are needed, the cost, etc. Then concerning the bus trip, we debate the size of the bus, what color it is, old or new, the driver, whether it is more economical or faster to take taxis instead, and more. While this continues, we forget all about Nigeria and the purpose of the trip. We get so heated in our disputes about airplanes and buses that we don't even want to go to Nigeria anymore. Our entire focus gets distracted, and the trip to Nigeria is no longer on anyone's mind.

In this allegory, going to a city in Nigeria is likened to God's eternal purpose of His ekklesia. The airplane and bus are likened to justification by faith and sanctification through the inner life of Christ. However, no matter how wonderful these two items are, they are simply procedures to arrive at God's eternal goal, which is the oneness of His people in Him. Yet today, believers are entirely focused on these two items and have lost track of their ultimate purpose. Additionally, amid all the disputes and confusion, especially over personal sanctification, believers have lost heart for ekklesia: the oneness of diverse believers.

As much as justification relieves us from the "works of the law" (i.e., "the just shall live by faith" which was Martin Luther's Reformational cry) and as much emphasis is placed upon the "Christ-life" and becoming a true follower of Jesus Christ (aka, *discipleship*) . . . these are but means to an ultimate end: His Ekklesia. If we do not know where, why, how, when, or the what of "all this" justification and sanctification, then the goal will be obscured, and we'll lose sight of His ultimate purpose in this universe! In other words, why are we evangelizing . . . then going through intense discipleship, effective sanctification if it does not result in the building up of His Ekklesia?

This book expounds on the above thesis.

The Lord's Ekklesia

> . . . and all the brothers who are with me, To the churches [*ekklesiai*] of Galatia . . . For you have heard of my former life in Judaism, how I persecuted the church of God violently and tried to destroy it.
>
> —Gal. 1:2, 13

> And I tell you, you are Peter, and on this rock, I will build my
> church [*ekklesia*], and the gates of hell shall not prevail against it.
> —Matt. 16:18

Paul addressed his letter to the *ekklesiai* (Gk. plural) throughout Galatia (Gal. 1:2). In God's plan, His ekklesia is composed of all His people in Jesus Christ. Universally, there is only one ekklesia of God (Eph 1:22-23). However, His *ekklesiai* are practically manifested among His diverse people in unity in any given city or community (Rev. 1:11). This is also patterned after the Greeks, where there is only one ekklesia per city, legislating for the entire city.

The Greek word "ekklesia" in the New Testament was purposely mistranslated in the English Authorized King James Version to the word "church," which literally means a building for worship[3]. Historically, this was done so that those who owned the churches (Roman or Anglican) could dictate their teachings/doctrines from these buildings, thereby exerting control through their interpretation of the Scriptures.

Since the sixteenth century many churches have been greatly used by the Lord to spread the gospel and teach the Bible throughout the earth. Nevertheless, every church has their own brand of doctrine and practice, causing believers in churches to segregate from believers outside of that specific confession/denomination. Therefore, without prejudice or judgment, the system of churches has caused confusion and division among God's people — either purposefully or inadvertently.

Today, all churches are essentially places where a particular ministry is conducted through one person or group of persons. However, the Lord's ekklesia does not belong to nor can it be controlled by any one ministry (pastors or ministers). It is God's people in a democratic assembly where believers from diverse perspectives and factions are in a "safe space" to worship and lift up Jesus Christ together — without conforming to a set of creedal restrictions aside from the very "doctrine of Christ" (2 John 8-11). Each person has the right and responsibility to share one-by-one their experiences and knowledge of Jesus Christ (1 Cor. 14:26-33). Though there may be believers in opposition concerning doctrinal, political, socio-economical viewpoints, they still love, support, and accept one another.

---

3   church | Search Online Etymology Dictionary (etymonline.com)

They are in one fellowship and respect each other's convictions. This is the ekklesia of the believers the Lord has assembled (1 Cor. 14:33).

Paul's heart and concern is for God's eternal purpose: the Lord's ekklesia.

Since Jewish Christians were teaching things which stumbled and divided believers (i.e., "preaching another gospel" — Gal. 1:9), Paul wrote specifically to all the *ekklesiai* throughout Galatia to expose these divisive teachings and uncover those with an agenda to divide the Body of Christ. Concerning this matter, Paul was in great travail like a laboring mother about ready to give birth (Gal. 4:19).

Paul was fighting to expose divisions for the building up of the Lord's ekklesia.

Paul's revelation concerning the Lord's ekklesia was so magnificent and significant that readers of his epistles would find them incredible — unless they, too, had received the same revelation from the Father. Here are just a couple of his many astonishing descriptions concerning the ekklesia:

> And he put all things under his feet and gave him as head over all things to the church [ekklesia], 23 which is his body, the fullness of him who fills all in all.
>
> —Eph 1:22-23

> Husbands, love your wives, as Christ loved the church [*ekklesia*] and gave himself up for her . . . This mystery is profound, and I am saying that it refers to Christ and the church [ekklesia].
>
> —Eph 5:25, 32

Truly, it takes a revelation (Eph. 1:17) for Christians to be impacted: the ekklesia is the Body of Christ, and it is for the ekklesia (Christ's bride) Jesus gave Himself to die!

> But Saul was ravaging the church [*ekklesia*], and entering house after house, he dragged off men and women and committed them to prison.
>
> —Act 8:3

Therefore, Paul points out that before he received the revelation of Jesus Christ, he was a persecutor of the ekklesia of God. His goal was to destroy the ekklesia. He didn't say he was a persecutor of Jesus Christ, believers, or Christians. Rather, Paul sought to destroy the ekklesia. It is God's ekklesia Satan wished to destroy because the ekklesia will defeat his domain (Matt. 16:18). Therefore, Saul being under Satanic influence was not persecuting Jesus Christ directly, nor Christians individually, but the Lord's ekklesia. This has been the real spiritual battle since the days of the apostles.

Saul's (i.e., Paul's) method of persecuting the ekklesia was to enter houses where the ekklesia was gathered and drag believers into prison. He didn't arrest individual believers at the temple (e.g., at "Solomon's Porch") or walking on the streets, but it was the ekklesia gathered in homes he sought to destroy (Acts 8:3). Today, most countries do not experience overt physical persecution. Nevertheless, Satan's full-time work, day and night, is destroying God's ekklesia by continually dividing believers in the Lord's ekklesia.

> And I heard a loud voice in heaven, saying, "Now the salvation and the power and the kingdom of our God and the authority of his Christ have come, for the accuser of our brothers has been thrown down, who accuses them day and night before our God.
> —Rev 12:10

Dividing believers destroys the ekklesia. A kingdom divided cannot stand (Luke 11:17). The word "accuse" in Greek is "*kategoreo.*" This word anglicized becomes "*categories,*" and the "accuser" is literally the categorizer. He is categorizing God's people "day and night" into as many categories as possible in order that believers will identify and label themselves by whatever category in which they find themselves. In so doing, they are divided from those who might have chosen an opposing category. "*Kategoreo*" came to mean "accuse" because of categorizing two groups as prosecutor and defendant. Therefore, these accusations are sourced in Satan but are indirectly perpetrated by the brethren themselves. Christians who have picked one category (self-identification) are the ones directly or indirectly accusing with enmity those Christians outside or in opposition to their chosen category.

Examples abound among Christians today. Some identify with a group that adheres to the doctrine of "once saved always saved." Another group holds the doctrine that Christians can lose their salvation, believing it is a choice. Accusations between these two groups have existed for over 500 years: each one accusing the other of being deceived and unscriptural. They simply refuse to gather together around Christ alone! Imagine how many categories Satan has created among Christians when rampant categorization occurs over matters of holiness, spiritual gifts, discipleship methods, race, politics, including the latest while writing this book: vax or anti-vax for Covid-19. These divisive accusations/categorizations can be so destructive to fellowship among believers wherein it is common for Christians in opposing factions to terminate all spiritual associations with one another.[4]

This was what happened in Antioch when Peter and those identified by Paul as "the circumcision" separated and broke off fellowship with the uncircumcised Gentile believers. The Lord's ekklesia was, for all intents and purposes, null and void — destroyed!

Another Gospel, Distorting the Gospel

I am astonished that you are so quickly deserting him who called you in the grace of Christ and are turning to a *different* gospel — not that there is another one, but there are some who trouble you and want to *distort* the gospel of Christ. But even if we or an angel from heaven should preach to you a gospel *contrary* to the one we preached to you, let him be accursed.

–Gal 1:6-8

Paul's first item of admonition was that they have deserted the grace of Christ and went in the direction of another gospel. However, it is not actually another gospel such as Hinduism or Buddhism. Rather, it was a distortion of the gospel of Jesus Christ. The gospel of Jesus Christ is simple and straightforward: Jesus Christ is God, the Son of God, who became a genuine man (manifested in the flesh), and as the God-man, He died, resurrected, and ascended as the Lord of all. Whosoever would receive this simple faith and call out to the Lord Jesus would be saved (Rom. 10:9-12).

---

4   It once was customary that those who held to "premillennialism" (the manifestation of the future 1,000-year reign of Christ on the earth) could gather for large "prophetic conferences" (the Niagara Conferences, USA) declaring the Second Coming of Christ, the Spirit-filled life of the believer, and commitment to world evangelization — regardless of their views on the timing of the "rapture of the Church." Today, such diversity of opinion on such timing is rigidly maintained with differences of opinion so stark that one "belief system" views the other as "apostate."

Jewish believers at the time believed in such a Jesus; however, some of them preached that Gentile believers also needed circumcision, the law of Moses, to be saved (Acts 15:1). They didn't reject the gospel of Jesus Christ. Instead, they **added** something else to the gospel of Jesus Christ: the law of Moses (specifically, circumcision). Therefore, the distortion or perversion of the gospel was Jesus Christ plus something else. This is serious. Paul said such ones should be cursed (Gk. "*anathema*")!

Most Christians may not pay much attention to such a severe warning in preaching "another gospel." Why? Because they focus on the "simple gospel" in which Jesus Christ is being preached — they have not considered the additions to this gospel of salvation and its immediate distortions. Many unbelievers reject the gospel not solely concerning the person and work of Jesus Christ. Rather, they are fearful of all the other requirements expected of them if they become a Christian. In other words, faith in Jesus Christ means they also have to live a certain lifestyle, change their behaviors, or even align politically in a certain way.

These extra considerations require something other than faith in Jesus Christ. If this is the case, then the distortion of the gospel is much more widespread than Christians realize. Many preachers throughout the world may be, knowingly or not, preaching a distorted, perverted, contrary, or different gospel.

However, Paul's concern was not for the distortion of the gospel going out to unbelievers, but that the distortion was being preached to believers, the followers of Jesus Christ, by well-intentioned but contrarians to the simplicity of the Gospel of the Grace of God (Acts 20:24). These Galatians first received the gospel from Paul. It was the pure gospel through faith in Christ alone they received "so great a salvation." The original gospel preached was good enough. No one can improve on it, not angels or even Paul himself. In fact, if anyone claims to have improved on the original gospel, it is a perversion — he said, let that person "be accursed" (Gal. 1:8).

This perversion of the gospel was not directed at unbelievers but to believers in the *ekklesiai* throughout Galatia. The perversion Paul was addressing was not concerning teaching Christians can now get drunk, commit fornication, lie, steal, or do other evils that "grace may abound." Ironically, the "perversion" was to follow what God had initially commanded in the Scriptures (e.g., circumcision). Yes, in the perspective of the New Covenant, preaching to fulfill what God commanded previously in Scripture became a perversion of the gospel — those who preached such a distorted gospel were adjudged as "accursed" (*anathema*).

Satan's first tactic for destroying the Lord's ekklesia was to utilize Saul to persecute the ekklesia by dragging believers to prison. That didn't work. In fact, it had the opposite effect. Through physical persecution, starting in Jerusalem, the ekklesia spread further and faster (Acts 8:1-4), scattering the seed of life everywhere. Therefore, Satan changed his tactic. Instead of physical persecution and outward opposition, he deceived and tricked Christians to distort the gospel using God's own commandments. The distortion of the gospel damaged the Lord's ekklesia by dividing her from within. This tactic has been so successful that the fragmentation of the Body of Christ has increased for nearly 2000 years until now.

2

DIVISION: THE RESULT OF DISTORTING THE GOSPEL

Source of the Judaizers:

> Then after fourteen years I went up again to Jerusalem with Barnabas, taking Titus (a Greek) along with me . . .. Yet because of false brothers secretly brought in — who slipped in to spy out our freedom that we have in Christ Jesus, so that they might bring us into slavery.
>
> ~Gal 2:1, 4

> But some men came down from Judea and were teaching the brothers, "Unless you are circumcised according to the custom of Moses, you cannot be saved." . . . But some believers who belonged to the party of the Pharisees rose up and said, "It is necessary to circumcise them (i.e., the Gentiles) and to order them to keep the law of Moses."
>
> ~Act 15:1, 5

In Galatians 2:1-10, Paul narrated his trip to Jerusalem. He went to Jerusalem because Jerusalem was where Jewish believers were teaching the distortion of the gospel. This trip corresponded to the "Council in Jerusalem" as recorded in Acts 15[5]. These "Judaizers" were believers from Jerusalem who taught Gentile believers that for their salvation they needed

---

5   There is controversy concerning the date when this epistle was written and whether it was to the north or south Galatia. This book has taken the traditional view: The date is around AD 53-54, after the council in Jerusalem in Acts 15. Nevertheless, whether it was before the Jerusalem council or after (around AD 50), it does not matter as far as the basic thesis of this book, which is that Galatians was written to solve the problem of division among believers. However, if it was written before the Jerusalem council then this author would apologize to apostle Peter for being too harsh on him. A good discussion for dating this epistle: The Date and Destination of Galatians | Bible.org

to be circumcised in accordance with the law of Moses. The "false" brothers
he references are better defined as "deceitful" brothers. They did not reject
Jesus Christ as their Savior. They were true believers in Jesus Christ, but they
were called "false," because they deceitfully came among Gentile believers
with an agenda of bringing them under the law of Moses, into slavery.

Paul went to Jerusalem, attempting to expose the Judaizers and prevent
them from preaching a distorted gospel. He hoped to deal with the source
of the problem and settle the matter both with the ekklesia in Jerusalem and
with the entire leadership of Jewish believers.

The Council in Jerusalem ended with a conclusion from James applying
a powerful prophecy from Amos addressing the dispute. James made a
decision not to trouble the Gentiles regarding the "yoke of circumcision"
(and the "apostles and elders" concurred — Acts 15:22-29). No longer
would the Gentiles be saddled with the law of Moses regarding circumcision
as a prerequisite to salvation. James concluded that Gentile believers
joining with the Jewish believers fulfills Amos' prophecy of rebuilding the
Tabernacle ("tent" or "booth") or the United Kingdom of David.

Since the Breach of Jeroboam, the Kingdom of David had been divided
and separated into the ten northern tribes of Israel and the two southern
tribes of Judah and Benjamin. After 19 kings over nearly 300 years, the
ten northern tribes of Israel (aka Jezreel, Ephraim, Samaria) were carried
off by the Assyrians and were swallowed up by the nations (Hos. 8:8).
Through the work of Jesus Christ, the Kingdom of David was being made
whole by joining the Jewish believers with the Gentile believers into one
united kingdom.

This prophecy in Amos 9:11-12 was being fulfilled right before their
eyes in the "here and now" with the Gentiles being included into the
Kingdom of David! Therefore, Gentile believers do not need to be Jewish,
nor do the Jewish believers need to be Gentiles. In the Body of Christ, there
is a distinction of individuals, even races and ethnic groups; yet there is ONE
BODY. (Note: there will be a further and in-depth discussion concerning
Acts 15 later in this book)

Division: The Result and Evidence of a Distorted Gospel.

With such a conclusion at the Jerusalem Council, trouble from preaching
"another gospel" by the Judaizers should have stopped. However, within
two to three years of this Council, Paul publicly rebuked Peter concerning
a similar matter when Peter showed up with Barnabas, and the Judaizers

from Jerusalem in Antioch, which is where the disciples were first called "Christians" (Acts 11:26).

Paul told the story in chapter two of Galatians, starting from verse 11. Jewish believers and Gentile believers were eating together and fellowshipping as the Lord's ekklesia. Some believers came from James in Jerusalem. When they showed up, Peter, "fearing the circumcision party," separated and divided from these Gentile believers and would not eat with them. Furthermore, as an influential apostle, all the other Jews including Barnabas, followed suit so that all the Jewish believers discontinued fellowship and were divided from the Gentile believers. Paul says: "The other Jews joined him (Peter) in his hypocrisy so that even Barnabas was led astray" (Gal. 2:13).

This is absolutely shocking! The same Peter who heard God's direct command to eat unclean things was now rebelling against this command. The same Peter who preached and witnessed the first Gentiles receiving the Holy Spirit in the house of Cornelius was rejecting these believers. The same Peter who passionately defended Gentile believers in the Jerusalem council was now betraying those whom he once defended. The same Peter to whom Jesus said: "I will build My church [ekklesia]" (Matt. 16:18). This Peter now finds himself fearful and weak concerning God's eternal purpose of the One Body of Christ. This shows the stronghold of how a previous understanding of God's Law in Scripture can and will continue to affect a person even though God has made the First Covenant obsolete and moved on to the New Covenant (Heb. 8:13).

Paul rebuked Peter openly in front of all with a forceful indictment stating Peter stood condemned and acted hypocritically. Paul's next accusation, a shocking unveiling: Peter had deviated from the truth of the gospel.

> But when Cephas [Peter] came to Antioch, I opposed him to his face because he stood condemned. For he regularly ate with the Gentiles before certain men came from James. However, when they came, he withdrew and separated himself because he feared those from the circumcision party. Then, the rest of the Jews joined his hypocrisy so that even Barnabas was led astray by their hypocrisy. But when I saw that they were deviating from the **truth of the gospel** . . .."
>
> –Gal 2:11-14

Paul juxtaposed "truth of the gospel" here with "distort the gospel" in chapter one. Peter's actions were against the very purpose and reality of the gospel of Jesus Christ — the very essence of the gospel of salvation and oneness of His ekklesia. This separation is the evidence or result of accepting another gospel or an overt perversion of the gospel. It wasn't an issue of salvation per se — it had everything to do with the denial of the work of the cross in "one new man in place of the two, so making peace" (Eph. 2:14-15).

It is critical to connect the dots here: The direct evidence of being influenced by "another gospel" is separation and division! Paul said those preaching a distorted gospel, "let him be accursed" (Gal. 1:8,9). Now we witness Peter opposing the truth of the gospel by separating himself from the uncircumcised believer. This division of hypocrisy was the result of a perverted gospel.

The Completion Gospel: Saved by Grace and Peace between Divided People

> Then one of them, named Caiaphas, who was high priest that year, spoke up . . . he prophesied that Jesus would die for the Jewish nation, and not only for that nation but also for the scattered children of God, to bring them together and make them one.
>
> —John 11:49, 51-52, NIV

> For he himself is our peace, who has made us both one and has broken down in his flesh the dividing wall of hostility by abolishing the law of commandments expressed in ordinances, that he might create in himself one new man in place of the two, so making peace, and might reconcile us both to God in one body through the cross, thereby killing the hostility. And he came and preached peace to you who were far off and peace to those who were near.
>
> —Eph 2:14-17

People are saved by grace through faith so that no one can boast (Eph. 2:8-9). This is possible because Jesus Christ died for our sins (1 Cor. 15:3). This understanding of the Christian faith for personal salvation is universally accepted among Christians of all denominations.

John shows us it is just as important that Jesus died to bring His scattered children into one by breaking down the middle wall of hostility between the two most divided people in history: Jews and Gentiles. It is through the cross that all barriers are torn down to create one New Man. The peace which brings forth unity must be preached. The good news must be spread and evangelized with this complete gospel message. Peace with God for salvation and peace among brethren made one by the same blood of His cross. Most Christians have neglected this cardinal aspect of the gospel of Christ!

Peter's act of separation clearly and directly contradicted and opposed the gospel of Jesus Christ. He became an enemy of the cross of Christ. He made the cross of Christ ineffective for unifying divided people by withdrawing from Gentile believers.

Many spiritually helpful biblical doctrines and practices divide believers. It is a distortion and perversion of the gospel when certain doctrines are regarded as essential for a believer's continual salvation. And, in the case of Peter, these doctrines are often grounds for separation from other believers. This is hypocrisy upon hypocrisy.

For example, there are followers of Jesus who truly believe in Jesus Christ, His death, and resurrection. They have accepted Him as their personal Savior, having confessed "Jesus is Lord" to the glory of God the Father. However, because of their church affiliation, they may not know the doctrine of justification by faith. Nevertheless, this person is still justified before God even though they don't know Romans 3:26-28. They are righteous before God even though they will probably go through unnecessary spiritual condemnation without the knowledge of justification by faith.

A person who has received the doctrine of justification by faith will experience spiritual freedom. However, he may then uplift this knowledge to an extent where he or she will demean those who have not come to such knowledge of the truth. Subsequently, this person may not extend fellowship to those believers in another church without this knowledge.

Consider another example: since the early twentieth century many Christians have received outward manifestations of the Spirit. One of these is the gift of tongues. Many believe this gift strengthens them to live a more holy and victorious Christian life. Some have been so focused on this doctrine and practice that they regard those lacking the experience of this gift are without the Spirit and possibly not even saved.

Even now, believers without such an experience push back and condemn these "Pentecostal" experiences to be out of the flesh and fake. More divisions have sprung up relating to the topic of living a victorious and holy Christian life. These factions can be so entrenched that many Christians do not have fellowship with each other due to these differences.

We need accurate and healthy knowledge of the truth, and we need nourishing teachings and practices. However, history has shown that without a revelation concerning the one "New Man" a full vision of His ekklesia with His diverse people in unity created through the cross — then many items can be added to this simple faith inevitably dividing the Body of Christ.

Nullifying Justification

> But when I saw that their conduct was not in step with **the truth of the gospel**, I said to Cephas before them all, "If you, though a Jew, live like a Gentile and not like a Jew, how can you force the Gentiles to live like Jews?" We ourselves are Jews by birth and not Gentile sinners; yet we know that a person is not justified by works of the law, but through faith in Jesus Christ, so we also have believed in Christ Jesus, in order to be justified by faith in Christ and not by [the] works of the law, because by works of the law no one will be justified. But if, in our endeavor to be justified in Christ, we too were found to be sinners, is Christ then a servant of sin? Certainly not! For if I rebuild what I tore down, I prove myself to be a transgressor.
>
> –Gal 2:14-18

The fact that Peter was eating with the Gentiles (which was prohibited by the Mosaic law) showed that he, including the Jewish believers with him, was living like a Gentile. God commanded Peter to eat with Gentiles since God has cleansed them (Acts 10:14, 28). Now that all Jewish believers withdrew and separated themselves, they found themselves "forcing" the Gentiles by saying: unless you become circumcised, to come under the law like us, we cannot fellowship with you.

One difficulty in understanding this concept is due to the words "sinner" and "sin." Most readers immediately revert to understanding sin in the moral sense. Such a sinner is one who does things such as lying, stealing, fornicating, etc. There is a disconnect between the rebuke of Peter for terminating fellowship with Gentile believers and the subsequent verses concerning justification. Most readers immediately connect justification by faith being related to our moral failures as sinners.

According to Galatians 2:15, the Jews at the time considered all Gentiles as sinners. They were sinners just for being a Gentile in nature, even if they didn't commit any immoral sins. Sin (Gk. *hamartia*) literally means "a missing of the mark" (Vine's). The Gentiles missed the mark by disregarding the law of Moses. It is at this point Paul said that no one is justified or made righteous before God by fulfilling the law. In fact, by laboring to fulfill the Mosaic law, no one can be justified. The only way to be justified is through faith in Christ Jesus.

Jewish believers thought that they were being righteous by separating themselves from the Gentiles, but actually they became condemned as transgressors.

One may believe that a person is righteous before God by faith in Jesus, which is true. However, what evidence do you have of your righteousness before God? If it is only in the unseen spiritual world that you are justified in Christ, then you can only be certain when coming before the throne of God on that day of judgment. What confidence does one have of their righteousness today? What is the evidence of such a matter of eternal consequence?

According to Paul in Galatians 2, the evidence of justification by faith looks like believers accepting into fellowship those who are different, even those considered *sinners* according to the law. Conversely, the evidence that you are **not** enjoying the reality of your justification by faith is your separation from those contrary to you. Joining in fellowship with all those who are justified by faith, whether Jews or Gentiles, is the result of justification by faith.

John said in 1 John 4:20: If anyone says, "I love God," and hates his brother, he is a liar; for he who does not love his brother whom he has seen cannot love God whom he has not seen

Applying this logic: anyone who says, "I am justified by faith," yet separates and divides from his brother is deceived. He who cannot receive in fellowship his brother, even one who is contrary, cannot have the assurance of being right with God whom he has not seen.

Why would Christ justify Jewish believers by faith and then ask them to join with sinners? Christ didn't do such a thing because, in the eyes of God, the Gentiles are no longer sinners. They have been justified by faith as well. The redemption of Christ is for all who put their faith in Him (Rom. 3:22-30).

When Jesus Christ died on the cross, He broke down the middle wall of hostility between Jews and Gentiles. He abolished the hatred between Jew and Gentile, a hatred which was compounded by hundreds of "rules and regulations." The cross of Christ did away with this hatred by nailing all such hatred, sin, and separation between Jew and Gentile to His cross.

> When you were dead in your trespasses and in the uncircumcision of your sinful nature, God made you alive with Christ. He forgave us all our trespasses, having canceled the debt ascribed to us in the decrees that stood against us. He took it away, nailing it to the cross!
>
> –Col. 2:13-14

Peter was the first in the New Testament to break down the wall between Jew and Gentile by fellowshipping and joining himself to the Gentiles at Cornelius' house (Acts 10). By separating himself from the Gentiles, he was rebuilding the wall of separation, thus becoming a transgressor against the cross of Christ, the gospel of Jesus Christ!

Died with Christ and the Indwelling Christ

> For through the law I died to the law so that I might live to God. I have been crucified with Christ. It is no longer I who live, but Christ who lives in me. And the life I now live in the flesh I live by faith in the Son of God, who loved me and gave himself for me. I do not nullify the grace of God, for if righteousness were through the law, then Christ died for no purpose.
>
> –Gal. 2:19-21

Galatians 2:20 has been the go-to verse for believers seeking to live a crucified life, one of self-denial, and bearing the cross. "I am crucified with Christ"; therefore, I can overcome all temptations of the flesh. In addition to this, "Christ lives in me"; thus, I can be holy and victorious. This is the sanctified life to most serious Christians: having victory over sin and worldliness with the ability to be humble and loving since Christ lives in them. This sanctified life has always been measured in an individual's experience for their personal salvation journey in holiness.

These verses are a continuation of Paul's rebuke of Peter for separating himself from Gentile believers. Peter and the rest of these Jewish believers divided or separated themselves from Gentile sinners based on the law of Moses in order to be righteous. It is with this in view that Paul said, "I am crucified with Christ." Since you (Jewish believers) are dead in Christ, you are no longer under the law which required you to be separated (Ex. 33:16; 1 Kings 8:53). The crucified life means a believer can now live to God and with his diverse brothers and sisters.

Living to God is identical to living according to God's desire. He desires the joining together of those previously divided into one New Man. He desires His ekklesia: diversity in unity. "Living to God" for Peter and the Jews meant staying in fellowship with these reprobate Gentile believers.

"No longer I who live": the Jewish identity and every other old identity of the "I" who lived is no longer . . . it has been terminated on the cross of Christ. Both the Jewish believers and the Gentile believers have Christ living in them. Whether circumcision or uncircumcision, whether according to law or outside of the law, they are one.

One may ask: What does sanctification or holiness look like in accordance with Galatians 2? It looks like one new man so making peace. It does not look like shutting-out oneness in isolation or with "spiritual peers" and declaring one is living the crucified life. A "follower of Christ" or "true discipleship" has nothing to do with becoming a "super-spiritual" holy person – No, it has to do with enjoying fellowship with all believers in the one New Man.

Since the same Christ lives in all kinds of different believers, no matter how contrary they may be to each other, there should only be one fellowship, one Body of Christ. Any believer who would withdraw themselves or terminate fellowship with any other believer is not identifying with both the crucified Christ and Christ living in them. The inverse would also be true. The evidence and result of living a life crucified with Christ and a life of "Christ in me" means a life of fellowship with all believers without separation from any.

Separating from other believers due to the law has essentially nullified the grace of God as though Christ died for nothing. This is a serious attack on the gospel! The gospel is to announce the effectiveness of Christ's death in saving believers by grace and peace. This includes the termination of the requirements contained in ordinances to bring peace between divided people (Eph. 2:14-16). The cross of Christ terminated the animosity, the hatred between peoples — this "hatred" swings both ways — hatred against Gentiles by the Jewish nation and hatred against Jews by the Gentile nations.

One may think that dividing over the Mosaic law is not relevant to most Christians. Although there may not be much debate over the actual Mosaic law, the principle of dividing over "righteousness, circumcision, and law" is exceedingly relevant today. It is the source of many divisions plaguing Christians. This book will provide contemporary examples showing how this cardinal emphasis found in Galatians remains applicable for solving the problem of today's divisions in the Body of Christ.

The oneness as described in this book is different than ecumenism which is an institutional effort to bring various church organizations (denominations) together. The oneness among believers described in this book is organic (versus organizational) between individual believers regardless of which church they may or may not attend. This organic oneness is based on what has been described in Galatians: faith in Jesus Christ, which afforded His believers justification and the supply of the Spirit.

3

BEGIN AND CONT
BY FAITH ALON

The Hearing of Faith

> O foolish Galatians! Who has bewitched you? It was before your eyes that Jesus Christ was publicly portrayed as crucified. Let me ask you only this: Did you receive the Spirit by works of the law or by hearing with faith? Are you so foolish? Having begun by the Spirit, are you now being perfected by the flesh? . . . Does he who supplies the Spirit to you and works miracles [inherent power] among you do so by works of the law, or by hearing with faith.
> –Gal 3:1-3, 5

What a judgment by Paul. He said the Galatians were "bewitched" by the Judaizers! According to *Thayer's Greek English-Lexicon*, the Greek word for "bewitched" can also be translated "traduce," which means: "shamed by means of falsehood" (Marriam-Webster). The Judaizers misrepresented the law and shamed the Galatians into using their flesh (self-effort) to fulfill the law. This is a subtle form of deceit, which all Christians need to recognize and reject. Therefore, any Christian being shamed for fellowshipping with other genuine believers in Christ is bewitched or traduced. Such distortion of the gospel bewitched these Galatian believers. This bewitching has a Satanic intention. The Satanic intention of preaching a different gospel complicates the simplicity of faith resulting in divided believers.

How does one understand "the hearing of faith?" Comparing all functions of a person, such as seeing, breathing, and eating, hearing is the only one that doesn't require effort. Even breathing requires some effort. When a person is extremely frail, a ventilator is needed to help them breathe. However, hearing requires no muscles or energy. Psychologists and medical professionals confirmed people in a coma can still hear and their bodies

...act. Hearing is the only function you cannot voluntarily stop. Even when a person closes their eyes and their mouth and voluntarily stops breathing, they cannot close their ears from hearing.

> ... the dead will hear the voice of the Son of God, and those who hear will live.
>
> −John 5:25
>
> So faith comes from hearing and hearing through the word of Christ.
>
> −Rom. 10:17

What a contrast faith is to the works of the law! "Works" require effort and expanding energy. Hearing of faith requires neither of these. The dead don't have the life or energy to do anything; yet, they can hear. The Son is speaking, and when the dead hear, they live, and they receive eternal life. Even the faith to believe didn't originate from the hearer. Such faith is a gift from God a hearer receives when listening to the words of Christ (Eph. 2:8; Rom. 10:17). This faith originated from Christ (Heb. 12:2). As a person hears the words of Christ or words concerning the person of Christ, the hearer receives faith. By this faith he or she believes in the crucified and resurrected Jesus Christ. By believing the "Christ portrayed crucified" the Spirit is received.

The gospel of Jesus Christ is a picture of the wonderful God who became flesh (man). Jesus died on the cross and was resurrected as the life-giving Spirit to be the full blessing of God to humanity. When an unbelieving person hears and visualizes this portrait of God, an appreciation and understanding of Jesus Christ fills his heart. Without any effort from this person faith is sparked or infused into his innermost being. Then he responds to Jesus in faith through a simple prayer or a cry out to His name. Just like that, the Spirit is received, and salvation activated.

The salvation given to humankind cannot be simpler or easier to access. However, the Judaizers bewitched the believers and brought them back to the works of the Old Covenant. What a deception! The gospel portrait Paul painted was Christ and Him crucified (1 Cor. 1:23). Paul said if even he deviates from preaching this gospel, he should be cursed. Through simple faith believers receive the Spirit; the Spirit in them was the resurrected Jesus Christ living in them (Gal. 2:20).

This simplicity of faith initiating the Christian journey includes justification (made righteous before God), being crucified with Christ, and living in union with the Spirit of Christ. They do not do anything more — zero — nothing else has been added. These Galatian believers had such an excellent beginning, but now they desired to use the effort of their flesh (self-effort) to follow the law to perfect themselves.

Paul maintained the only way to grow and be perfected (full-grown) in the Christian journey was to persist by the same faith in Jesus Christ. Believers are continually being supplied by the Spirit for their entire journey in the same way of faith. This occurs without doing work according to the laws of God in order to be made righteous or holy. The Spirit Himself will fully complete and equip believers in Christ.

Every Christian had their beginning by faith. Faith is the only way to begin. However, during their long Christian journey, most will revert to the works of the law to perfect themselves. When they start struggling with failures in holiness, shortages in victories, and lack of devotion, they start trying harder by exerting more and more effort. They regress to the Old Covenant by the works of the law. Paul stressed there is only one way they start their life with Christ: by faith. Similarly, there is only one way to continue their journey with Christ: by faith.

The supply of the Spirit includes an inherent power. The Greek word for "miracles" in verse 5 is *"dynamis,"* which means "inherent power, power residing in a thing by virtue of its nature" (Thayer's). Certainly, there is inherent supernatural power within God. However, the focus here is the indwelling power of the Spirit within believers, not miraculous power which God is directly responsible for performing. Instead, it is the innate power generated by the supply of the Spirit within the believer. This understanding is supported by Eph. 3:16, "He may grant you to be strengthened with power (*dynamis*) through his Spirit in your inner being." Therefore, the believers' inner man is strengthened with the innate power of the Spirit.

And [you may know] what is the immeasurable greatness of his power [*dynamis*] toward us who believe, according to the working of his great might that he worked in Christ when he raised him from the dead and seated him at his right hand in the heavenly [places].

–Eph 1:19-20

> But we have this treasure in jars of clay, to show that the surpassing power [*dynamis*] belongs to God and not to us. We are afflicted in every way, but not crushed; perplexed, but not driven to despair; persecuted, but not forsaken; struck down, but not destroyed; always carrying in the body the death of Jesus, so that the life of Jesus may also be manifested in our bodies.... So, death is at work in us, but life in you.
>
> –2 Cor. 4:7–10, 12

Followers of Christ have an inherent power (*dynamis*) within them: the power of resurrection and ascension. It is not the supernatural power of creation but the power that flourishes in the midst of hardships and challenges. This is the power that overcomes death. The same power seated Christ in the heavenlies and subjected all things under His feet (Eph. 1:22). This power is unleashed only through death.

Paul experienced this power when he suffered for the sake of the gospel. Christ being the treasure in Him is the inherent power (cf. Gal. 2:20). This power was manifested through all kinds of challenges and difficulties in Paul's life. Instead of showing bitterness and complaining, life was given to those witnessing and hearing the gospel. This is the same power supplied to believers through the hearing of faith.

Understanding this can have a profound effect on Christian experiences. Most believe they need more faith in order to miraculously change their environment. Their focus of "faith" is for God to perform supernatural acts. However, Paul is referencing the power generated from within believers themselves. This power is IN believers, not outside. Supernatural healing, miracles, or foreseeing the future is not the primary function of this power. Instead, it is the power to transform the nature of a person from within: from anxiety to comfort, from discouragement to joy, from fear to love, and from condemnation to forgiveness. This power is the source of the fruit of the Spirit in Galatians 5:22.

All these uniquely wonderful attributes of Jesus such as love, kindness, diligence, boldness, forgiveness, peacemaking, and much more, are supplied by the Spirit. These attributes are what the innate and inherent power produces in every believer through faith. It seems counterintuitive, but the more effort believers exert to display these attributes, the more they experience resentment, disappointment, and discouragement. The only way to produce the fruit of the Spirit is to remain in faith. We must continue looking to, appreciating, and abiding in fellowship with Jesus.

Living under the Law Is a Curse

> For all who rely on works of the law are under a curse; for it is written, "Cursed be everyone who does not abide by all things written in the Book of the Law, and do them." Now it is evident that no one is justified before God by the law, for "The righteous shall live by [out of] faith."
>
> —Gal 3:10-11

The Judaizers' goal was for Gentile Christians to become righteous according to law; thus, by doing this, they caused a division. Paul defines the law as "all the things written in the Book." These "things written" certainly include the Ten Commandments and its ancillary ordinances relating to morality and ceremonial worship. The book of the law can easily extend to many more commandments made for Christians in the New Testament. Therefore, there are even more laws for Christians to abide by in their living. This body of laws is so great it can at times seem conflicting. Most Christians pick and choose which laws to obey and which to ignore. However, James tells us if one law is broken, then all are broken (James 2:10).

Consider this sample list of various laws Christians attempt to fulfill in addition to the Ten Commandments:

- Turn the other cheek.
- Do not have anxiety.
- Don't look at anyone with sexual lust.
- Don't call anyone a "fool."
- Give to the poor.
- Pray unceasingly.
- Love your enemies.
- Submit to your husband.
- Forgive those who wrong you repeatedly.
- Don't be lukewarm.
- Honor those whom you may disdain.
- Don't give any appearance of sin.

- Cover a woman's head in worship.
- Go preach the gospel.
- This list of "laws" goes on and on.

When Christians live by the works of these or any other laws, not only are they living under a curse, but they also judge other Christians who do not live up to their standard of their chosen law. One visible result of such critical and condemning attitude is when those who have followed the law of their choosing divide from those who are not up to their standard or have chosen a different set of laws. However, whichever set of laws one chooses as a measurement for righteousness, the reality remains: No one can abide by all the laws. Therefore, working to fulfill a chosen standard of righteous living by keeping laws is an effort that becomes a curse.

For example, one group of Christians may decide their standard of showing righteousness is being exemplary in a life of holiness: no swearing, modesty for women, no sexual sins, no drinking of alcohol, giving to the poor, and not conforming to the trend of the world. Another group may have a much looser standard of morality, but they focus on forgiveness, honoring those disdained in society, and aggressively preaching the gospel through contemporary music. Due to their diverse standard of righteousness according to law, these two groups may view each other with contempt resulting in separation from fellowship. Each group may even consider the other group to be "enemies" of the gospel. However, neither fulfilled all the laws: namely, "love your enemies." This failure resulting in division among believers would mean both groups are under a curse.

Christians are often very quick and harsh in judging others, especially other believers. Their actions are evidence they are still using the law, either the Mosaic law or the laws in the New Testament, as their standard for judgment. They have not understood that "the righteous shall live by faith." Believers do not only begin their Christian life by faith, but they continue to live for the rest of their lives by and out of faith. Righteousness belongs to those who live in constant fellowship with the Lord in Spirit, not to those who do their best to live according to law.

The Blessing of Abraham for both Jews and Gentiles

The focus of faith in this chapter is not merely to trust that God will take care of our physical existence and spiritual needs. Faith is the channel for believers to engage with God's Spirit. It is through faith Christians have fellowship with Jesus Christ, who dwells in their hearts (Eph. 3:17). Faith then is the gift from God through which believers receive Him, know Him, fellowship with Him, and are filled with Him.

Paul then used Abraham to declare righteousness by faith is not based on law. God justified Abraham by faith 430 years before the law was given by Moses. God counted him as righteous simply because He believed God's promise — before circumcision (Rom. 4:5, 21). Clearly, righteousness before God had nothing to do with fulfilling the law since it was not given until centuries later. In other words, faith alone is the only requirement to be justified before God. Abraham didn't do anything else other than believe God's promise.

> Then the LORD appeared to Abram and said, "To your offspring [seed] I will give this land." So he built there an altar to the LORD, who had appeared to him.
>
> –Gen 12:7
>
> And in your offspring shall all the nations of the earth be blessed, because you have obeyed my voice.
>
> –Gen 22:18
>
> So that in Christ Jesus the blessing of Abraham might come to the Gentiles, so that we might receive the promised Spirit through faith . . .. 16 Now the promises were made to Abraham and to his offspring. It does not say, "And to offsprings," referring to many, but referring to one, "And to your offspring," who is Christ.
>
> –Gal 3:14, 16

Additionally, the promise God made to Abraham was to his **Seed** (offspring). This promise included the good land. Abraham's offspring (seed) was to inherit the good land. Simultaneously, in his offspring, "all the nations of the earth would be blessed."

Paul made two interpretations here in Galatians. First, he equated the promised physical good land as the Spirit in the New Covenant when he said, "receive the promised Spirit through faith." All that God is, and all that Jesus Christ accomplished is now included in the Spirit. The Spirit includes all the various descriptions: Holy Spirit, Spirit of God, Spirit of Christ, Spirit of Jesus Christ, Spirit of truth, Spirit of life, and Spirit of glory. This is the real and ultimate promised blessing upon God's people. The promised physical land was a type or foreshadowing of the real blessing upon God's people: the Spirit for their possession and enjoyment (See Hebrews 4).

In the Hebrew Scriptures, the good land is described as a land of riches, flowing with milk and honey, in which God's people will eat and drink without scarcity and have no lack (Deut. 8:7-10). It is a vast land covering as far as the eye can see and as much as their feet can walk in all directions. A land so vast God's people cannot get out of it and so rich they will be satisfied with enjoyment. Whether they do something good or something terrible, they are still in the good land. The real good land is the Spirit. Believers are enveloped by the Spirit in which they are enclosed. The Spirit is the believers' entire environment. All the riches of Christ are available for their enjoyment, where there is no scarcity, and they have no lack. Therefore, like the good land, believers are told to walk in Him and be rooted in Him (Col. 2:6-7). Both the Spirit and the good land are only received through faith.

After accepting that they are justified by faith, many Christians think they need to earn or work to stay in fellowship with Christ. They fear they will be outside the realm of Christ if they fall into temptation and fail. Some may hold a teaching that after they fall into "sin," they will need to do "penance" for a period of time before God accepts them back. Most feel they will at least suffer judgment from God, or should remain shameful for a period before they can continue their fellowship with God or others. Those holding this view do not yet realize they are surrounded by the Spirit from which exit is impossible. Some may fail to the extent of breaking the law resulting in imprisonment. However, even in prison, they are still surrounded by the Spirit. Christ is there to supply them and be their enjoyment. The Spirit (the good land) is made real in their entire journey only through faith.

Second, Paul said that Abraham's offspring is singular Seed; not seeds (Gal. 3:16). Therefore, this offspring or Seed is Jesus Christ, alone. Jesus Christ is the real promised seed of Abraham. Therefore, it is Christ as the promised offspring Who will receive the promised Spirit. Indeed:

> So, in Christ Jesus you are all children of God through faith, for all of you who were baptized into Christ have clothed yourselves with Christ. There is neither Jew nor Gentile, neither slave nor free, nor is there male and female, for you are all one in Christ Jesus . . . If you belong to Christ, then you are Abraham's seed, and heirs according to the promise."
>
> –Gal. 3:26-29

Faith in Jesus Christ transferred believers into Christ. Before faith, people were outside of Christ. They were in the old Adam and the old creation. However, through faith believers are transferred into Christ. The writers of Acts and the epistles continually remind their readers that believers are IN Christ. Since they are in Christ, they are in the position to receive the promised Spirit. The only one way into Christ is by and through faith.

Throughout the New Testament, the writers use the phrase, "believes in Him (Christ)" by translating the Greek word "*eis*" as "in." According BDAG Lexicon, "*eis*" could and perhaps should be translated "into," as in: "believes *into* Him." Similarly, Thayer's first definition of "*eis*" is "of a place entered, or of entrance into a place, into." Paul would have used the Greek word "*en*" if he meant "in," rather than "*eis*." There is a significant difference between believes "in" and believes "into." When a person says, "Do you believe in me?" or "I believe in you," typically refers to a belief in the person's ability. Joe may say, "Do you believe I can swim a mile?" A reply could be: "I believe in you; you can do it." However, believing "into" can only be applied to the person of Christ. "Into" means it is through faith a believer is transferred into Christ. It is through faith Christians are now in the sphere and realm of Christ.

> "For God so loved the world, that he gave his only Son, that whoever believes in [into] him should not perish but have eternal life.
>
> –John 3:16
>
> I have come into the world as light, so that whoever believes in [*eis* or into] me may not remain in [*en*] darkness.
>
> –John 12:46

When we apply this concept to John 3:16 we discover it is through believing into Him people do not perish but have eternal life. Prior to believing into Him, they were outside of Him and in the condemned world. However, through believing, they came into Christ, into the realm and into the person of Jesus Christ. It is much more than believing in Christ's ability that He can save. Through faith, they entered into the good land of Christ, the Spirit. John 12:46 makes this distinction clearer: those who believe into Christ are now in the realm of Christ. They are no longer in the realm of darkness. People were in darkness, but through faith, they left the realm of darkness and entered into Christ in whom they now remain.

The scriptures declared: ". . . in your offspring shall all the nations of the earth be blessed." Not just Isaac's, Jacob's, and the twelve tribes of Israel, but all the nations. In this one offspring, all the nations are blessed. People from every tribe, language, nation are now included in Christ. While Jewish believers thought that they were special and chosen, Paul brought them back to Abraham to show, contrarily, they were the same as everyone else in Christ.

Paul then made a side note concerning why the law was given. God gave it to drive people to Christ. The law was not the problem; the problem was that people were dead in sin. The law was given as a guardian or a pedagogue/tutor to usher people into Christ. Once they are in Christ, the law's function has fulfilled its purpose and is no longer needed because they are now in the Lord Jesus Christ, who has fulfilled the law. Believers in Christ no longer need the law as their tutor.

Faith Alone Results in One Corporate Christ

> . . . for in Christ Jesus you are all sons of God, through faith. For as many of you as were baptized into Christ have put on Christ. There is neither Jew nor Greek, there is neither slave nor free, there is no male and female, for you are all one in Christ Jesus. And if you are Christ's, then you are Abraham's offspring, heirs according to promise.
>
> –Gal 3:26-29

Paul concludes that those who have believed into Christ are now immersed (baptized) in Him. The word "baptized" means immersed or completely enveloped in a sphere. That is the significance of water baptism:

it is a declaration that believers are immersed into the Trinity: Father, Son, and Holy Spirit, encircled, and never to get out of Him (Matt. 28:19).

Now, in Christ, there is no separation or division among people of distinctions that may be poles apart since they are ONE in Christ Jesus. On the one hand, Abraham's offspring is an individual named Jesus Christ. On the other hand, this Seed is a corporate Seed consisting of Jews and Greeks, male and female, slaves and free: a singular Seed consisting of a diverse people. Christ is now the corporate Christ with Jesus as the Head, and His diverse people as the Body: both the Head and the Body are Christ (1 Cor. 12:12).

Jews and Greeks are considered opposing people groups in terms of religion and culture, the battle of the sexes is more pronounced than ever; and master and slave couldn't be further apart in the social and economic order of things. Yet, each of these polar opposites are one in Christ. What a shock this is to the divisive and fractured world! This oneness is the result of Christ's death and resurrection and those who have entered the realm of Christ, the Spirit, through the simple faith. This gospel is truly good news to this world that is increasing in division and hate among those who are different from one another.

Consider how this epistle begins: Paul warned the Galatians concerning the perversion or distortion of the gospel of Jesus Christ. This distortion taught by some Jewish believers (Judaizers) was that in addition to faith in Jesus Christ, the Gentiles needed to keep the Mosaic law. Paul strongly condemned those who would distort the gospel to be cursed — anathema!

In chapter 2, Paul gave his readers evidence of someone influenced by a distorted gospel: Peter led Jewish believers who were present in Antioch to separate from fellowshipping with their Gentile counterparts. Paul openly condemned Peter's action as "against the truth of the gospel." Therefore, Peter's action resulted from the direct influence of "another gospel." Peter's division and segregation openly negated justification by faith, crucifixion with Christ, and the indwelling Jesus in His believers. Grace disappeared in that factious environment. This would imply Christ died in vain since His death was designed and intended to bring divided people into one (*i.e.,* unity).

Then in chapter 3, Paul admonished the Galatians, telling them they begin uniquely by faith and are to continue only by faith. He made an

irrefutable assertion that Abraham was counted righteous before God by
faith alone. It was through this faith; his offspring received the blessing of
his faith centuries before the law was given. He ended this chapter with a
powerful conclusion: Faith in Jesus Christ makes all diverse individuals who
are polar opposites one in Him. The oneness of God's uniquely different
people powerfully proclaims Jesus Christ's completed crucifixion and
resurrection work was designed to produce His ekklesia.

4

UNDERSTANDING AND SOLVING THE PROBLEM OF DIVISIONS

Circumcision: Chosen and Set Apart

When Peter, along with these Jewish believers, separated and cut off fellowship with the Gentile believers in Galatians 2, he was "fearing the circumcision party" (Gal. 2:12). This "circumcision party" consisted of those who bore the mark of circumcision: Thereby showing they were special because they were conformed to the law of Moses and separated from the uncircumcised.

Circumcision was a physically observable mark on a man's body, whereby someone could identify him as a Jew in compliance to the law of Moses. It was an unmistakable mark of distinction between a Jew and a Gentile. When a Gentile desired to convert to Judaism, they were required to be circumcised and thus bear the mark indicating they were adhering to the law of Moses.

Circumcision began with Abraham. It was the sign of a covenant made with Abraham. This covenant was created when God promised Abraham the second time, he would have a son (called Isaac). God required Abraham and his generation of offspring to bear this mark of circumcision.

> This is my covenant, which you shall keep, between me and you and your offspring after you: Every male among you shall be circumcised. You shall be circumcised in the flesh of your foreskins, and it shall be a sign of the covenant between me and you. He who is eight days old among you shall be circumcised. Every male throughout your generations, whether born in your house or bought with your money from any foreigner who is not of your offspring,
>
> —Gen. 17:10-12

God already counted Abraham (i.e., Abram) as righteous before Him when Abraham believed God's promise of an offspring thirteen years earlier (Gen. 15:6-7). Therefore, the covenant of circumcision was not the original covenant made with Abraham: He would have an offspring who would receive and possess the good land of Canaan (Gen. 15:18-21).

Since circumcision was a covenant with God, those circumcised would have a daily reminder for the rest of their lives that they are special before God. This unique mark would physically separate them from the uncircumcised. The word *holy* or *sanctify* means "to be set apart" or "separated." Therefore, circumcision was the sign of holiness or sanctification. The circumcised bear a mark of holiness. For this reason, the uncircumcised Gentiles were classified by the Jews as sinners. Without the mark of holiness, they would be considered as "unholy" (Gal. 2:15).

Therefore, circumcision was a mark of a covenant and consecration with God showing holiness and sanctification. These Jewish believers in Jesus Christ boasted of this mark and desired the Gentiles to bear the same mark to distinguish them as holy just as the Jewish Christians considered themselves.

Baptism Replaced Circumcision in the New Testament

In the New Testament, circumcision as a physical sign of a covenant was replaced by baptism.

> In him also you were circumcised with a circumcision made without hands, by putting off the body of the flesh, **by the circumcision of Christ, having been buried with him in baptism,** in which you were also raised with him through faith in the powerful working of God, who raised him from the dead.
>
> –Col 2:11-12

The apostle Paul used circumcision as a metaphor to describe an act of putting off the flesh. The flesh in the New Testament generally referred to the negative aspect of fallen humanity. When God created man's body, there was no sin in his body. But after eating the forbidden fruit, man fell from his "very good" place, becoming *flesh*, the dwelling place of sin (Gen. 1:31; Rom. 7:18; 8:3). Fleshly man could not please nor submit to God (Rom. 8:7-8).

Jesus Christ's crucifixion was God's way of cutting off sinful flesh. It was on the cross that the fallen flesh was terminated and buried so that humanity could be righteous in the eyes of God. The flesh in Romans 6 was called the "old man." This old man was crucified with Christ (Rom. 6:6, 19). Therefore, baptism was the physical symbol of what Christ did in His death and resurrection: the flesh, fallen humanity, is dead and buried — those who died in Christ were also resurrected with Him to live by the new life of God.

Baptism is the physical symbol of spiritual circumcision, but unlike circumcision, it does not leave a visible mark on a person. It is an event that takes place after faith in Christ. Just as Abraham was counted righteous before God at the time of his faith, believers in the New Covenant are also immediately saved, justified, and born anew at the moment of faith in Jesus Christ (Eph 2:8-9; Rom. 3:26; 10:8). Similarly, as Abraham's circumcision took place years after faith, the act of baptism also takes place after faith in Jesus Christ. The difference is that while circumcision leaves a mark on a man for the rest of his life, separating him from the uncircumcision, baptism does not leave such an external mark of separation.

"Circumcision" a Mark of Consecration and Holiness

Just as Jewish believers desired to bear a mark of covenant and holiness, Christians today may desire the same. Christians have displayed various marks to show covenant with God and holiness. A covenant in the Old Testament for Christians may be considered a kind of dedication or consecration to God. Some marks Christians display include:

- The way women dress (modest or not)
- Hairstyle (short or long hair for men)
- Music genre (classical, soft rock, or hard rock and rap)
- Movies they watch (PG or R)
- Smoking or not
- Car brands (practical or flashy)
- Not wearing jewelry

Then there are the more subtle spiritual marks such as: speaking in tongues, vocal support of a particular political party or social cause, wearing a crucifix, etc. The fact is that Christians have made various symbols, styles, and practices a sign of "circumcision" to differentiate themselves from the "sinners" (the uncircumcised).

It seems every church brand has an identifying mark to show both insiders and outsiders that a person is an adherent of a specific church. Typically, Christians who become members of any church long enough will bear an identifying mark of that church. It could be a dress code, a doctrinal understanding, a way of accepting or expressing spiritual gifts, even activism for a political party or social issue.

Just as circumcision was promoted based on Scriptures, every church with its "circumcision" showing consecration and holiness also uses Scriptures. Here are just a few examples:

- Women should dress with modesty and head-covering (1 Tim. 2:9; 1 Cor. 11:6)
- Men should not have long hair (1 Cor. 11:14)
- A Christian shouldn't keep up with modern trends in apparel, music genre, etc. (Rom. 12:2)
- Those filled with the Spirit should manifest the gift of tongues (Acts 2:4)
- Christians should wear a crucifix (1 Cor. 1:23)

Not only was circumcision commanded by God, supposedly, it also had health benefits (medical professionals generally accept this). Similarly, a modern Christian's sign of "circumcision" may have Scriptural grounds that benefit a Christian's spiritual journey. Therefore, the problem is not with circumcision nor following the law of Moses; the issue is when believers use circumcision (or choose not to be circumcised) to segregate and divide.

Similar to how the circumcised separated from fellowship with the uncircumcised, modern Christians may separate from other believers who do not bear the same mark. Many Christians have witnessed or been party to the following scenarios:

John is a committed member of a church that opposes drinking alcoholic beverages in any social setting considering it as unholy or unsanctified. His church believes those consecrated to God must abstain from drinking. John got together with a few other Christians who did not have the conviction that drinking a beer or two was "unholy." John being polite, accepted a beer when offered at the restaurant. When John saw a few church members coming into the restaurant, he quickly pushed his beer away and felt uncomfortable with those drinking beer. Shortly after that, he left his Christian friends and sat at the table with his fellow church members.

Jill is a member of a "spirit-filled" church with a certain moral conviction leading them to advocate for a particular political party. They would promote "speaking in tongues" is needed to manifest the fulness of the Spirit and as a sign of holiness. Additionally, they believe a person consecrated to God would fight for a just cause as a representative of God's kingdom. Due to this reasoning, she would not go to any church which does not speak in tongues, nor would she have fellowship with any Christians who support an opposing political party. Additionally, when she speaks to those who hold a view contrary to her beliefs, her agenda is to convert them to adopt her convictions.

These Christian practices whereby churches adopt and advocate for a particular expression of consecration to God aspire to keep a standard of holiness. There are hundreds of doctrinal understandings affecting various practices. All these become a mark of "circumcision" whereby Christians attempt to convert other believers to come under their brand of holiness. If they are not willing to convert to such a brand, they will be (in essence) considered as "uncircumcised" in their eyes. Furthermore, those focused on converting these "uncircumcised sinners" see little value in having fellowship with the unconverted.

It is apparent that a form of circumcision being used to divide believers is still very valid and persistent among Christians. This covenant mark and holiness may not be physical circumcision as with the first-century Jewish Christians, but having a mark identifying oneself with a particular brand of Christianity is still common among most followers of Jesus.

The problem Paul addressed in Galatians was not who is marked or unmarked. Rather, the crisis was that these marks were used to divide believers. It is unavoidable to have certain convictions while living a consecrated and holy life. Therefore, there's nothing wrong with bearing such signs. Instead, this is Paul's battle: bearing a mark should not be a determining factor for fellowship and oneness in the Body. For example, one may prefer to "eat kosher," but once that becomes a "distinctive" which separates fellowship from other believers you have "crossed the line."

Every believer is crucified with Christ and has Christ living in them. Whether one bears a mark or not, all are justified by faith in Jesus Christ. Therefore, every believer should come back to the truth of the gospel (Gal. 2:5, 14) where they are one in Christ. And they should stop letting their diverse convictions separate them from the one fellowship which all believers in Christ share.

Circumcision Is of the Heart

> For no one is a Jew who is merely one outwardly, nor is circumcision outward and physical. But a Jew is one inwardly, and circumcision is a matter of the heart, by the Spirit, not by the letter. His praise is not from man but from God.
>
> —Rom 2:28-29

Circumcision is a matter of the heart. It is no longer physical. Cutting off of the old man (the flesh) happens in the believer's heart by the working of the Spirit. Unlike any physical mark of circumcision, believers of Jesus Christ do not need such a mark because it is neither visible nor observable since it is in the heart. True holiness is not something demonstrated outwardly but inwardly in the heart of the believer.

God wants to cut our allegiance to everything in our hearts relating to the flesh and the fallen man. A circumcised heart is a pure heart (Matt. 5:8): a heart that loves God and God's eternal purpose with His people (Matt. 22:37; 24:48). While outward circumcision can become a mark of division, a circumcised heart is in unity with all believers (Acts 4:32). What a difference!

The Lord Jesus, during his time on earth, did not bear any outward signs or marks that would separate Him from a typical Jew. He was no different from common people (Mark 6:3; Luke 4:30). He ate and drank with tax collectors and sinners (Luke 7:34, 5:30). He stayed in rich people's homes (Luke 19:2-5). He allowed a sinful woman to kiss His feet after washing them with her tears and hair (Luke 7:37-38). Jesus lived broadly and inclusively with sinners because He was circumcised in His heart. These things can be problematic to people of the flesh. Their hearts can quickly be drawn away by temptations causing them to fall into sin. Jesus, with His heart circumcised, had no craving for the attractions of this world. He could not be enticed (Matt. 4:8-10). Therefore, He was liberated to mingle and associate Himself with all kinds of people.

Jesus did not outwardly live in a way that separated Him from sinners. He mingled with them, and they loved to be with Him. The religious people wanted physical separation as a sign of holiness (Mark 2:16). That was the point of circumcision: to separate from sinners. However, Jesus, who is uniquely the embodiment of true holiness, had the freedom to be with all types of people. Being holy was not an act or an event for Jesus. His very being was holy. He lived out holiness. Additionally, He died, resurrected, and became the life-giving and indwelling Spirit living in His believers so they, too, would be circumcised in their hearts (1 Cor. 15:45; 2 Cor. 3:17).

Similarly, since Paul's heart was circumcised, he could freely join himself with diverse groups of people without being entangled by any. In 1 Corinthians 9:19-22, Paul said he could be "all things to all people" to share the gospel with its blessings. Though a circumcised Jew, Paul didn't let that alienate him from anyone, including uncircumcised sinners. He was flexible and not pigeon-holed into one group. Therefore, he could be accepted by all groups.

Don't misunderstand: If God convicts a person to avoid certain people or places, or if the Spirit leads a person not to drink alcohol or dress in a certain way, then that person should obey and follow God. It is one thing to live in a way that the Spirit leads, but it is another to use this as a standard to compare, judge, and separate from those without a similar leading or conviction.

> One man esteems one day above another: another esteems every day alike. Let every man be fully persuaded in his own mind.
>
> –Rom. 14:5

The point is this: no matter how Christians practice their faith in Christ, it is the faith with which they are justified before God, crucified with Christ, and He lives in them. Those believers who live with this reality will not separate themselves from fellowship with believers who act contrary to them in consecration or holiness. Does this mean Christians should have no regard for falling or living in sin? No! Paul addresses this in the later chapters of Galatians.

A Slave Through the Work of the Flesh

> . . . For we say that faith was counted to Abraham as righteousness. How then was it counted to him? Was it before or after he had been circumcised? It was not after, but before he was circumcised. He received the sign of circumcision as a seal of the righteousness that he had by faith while he was still uncircumcised. The purpose was to make him the father of all who believe without being circumcised, so that righteousness would be counted to them as well.
>
> –Rom 4:9-11

Let's be clear: circumcision was not the reason for righteousness. Abraham was not counted righteous because of circumcision. Before Abraham was circumcised, he was already justified by faith before God. Therefore, God could say ". . . that in Abraham all the nations of the earth shall be blessed" (Gen. 18:18). These nations extend further than Isaac, Jacob, and the twelve tribes of Israel (the circumcised). Everyone among the nations (the uncircumcised), who has the same faith as Abraham, would receive the same blessing. They, too, are justified by faith.

> For it is written that Abraham had two sons, one by a slave woman and one by a free woman. But the son of the slave was born according to the flesh, while the son of the free woman was born through promise. Now this may be interpreted allegorically: these women are two covenants. One is from Mount Sinai, bearing children for slavery; she is Hagar. Now Hagar is Mount Sinai in Arabia; she corresponds to the present Jerusalem, for she is in slavery with her children.
>
> –Gal 4:22-25

Abram (Abraham) received God's promise of a seed that would be his heir in Genesis 15, and because he believed, God counted Abram "righteous" before Him (Gen. 15:6). Even though Abraham believed, he was not patient in receiving God's promise. Therefore, in Genesis 16, Abraham agreed to Sarah's proposal to have a child through her slave, Hagar. Abraham believed God and was justified (counted righteous). Yet, he couldn't wait for God's timing or schedule, so Abraham decided to fulfill God's promise by the effort of his flesh.

Through his own effort, Abraham did produce a son, Ishmael, by Hagar, but God didn't recognize Ishmael as the promised seed. When God came to Abraham thirteen years later, He told Abraham that Ishmael could not be his heir (Gen. 17:19-21). Again, God promised Abraham a seed that would be his heir. At this second time of promising, God gave Abraham the covenant of circumcision. Since then, all of Abraham's decedents, through both Ishmael and Isaac, were circumcised according to this covenant. Yet, Abraham was already counted righteous by God thirteen years earlier.

As with Abraham, we do not need to do anything more than have faith in God's promise of a Seed (Jesus Christ; Gal. 3:19) to be justified. It is the simple faith in Jesus Christ, without fulfilling any other command or requirements, that makes all believers in Christ righteous before God.

What Abraham did to produce a son for himself through a slave can be applied to the experience of modern Christians. After coming to faith in Christ, most Christians desire to be delivered from sin's power and become more like Jesus. They want to be immediately freed from all entangling distractions of the world, reasoning, "Didn't Jesus say, 'Be perfect as your heavenly Father is perfect' (Matt. 5:48)?" Reading the Scriptures, they realized they should no longer be angry, lustful, anxious, selfish, but loving, patient, generous, forgiving, and exercising self-control.

They view all of the attributes of Christ as requirements of the law. Now they are expected to fulfill these demands. When they fail at these standards, they become self-condemning and disappointed. Since growth takes time, most do not have the patience to wait for the indwelling Spirit of life to transform their heart and nature from within (Rom. 8:4). Being impatient, they try to work out these godly characteristics by their own efforts instead of being transformed according to God's timing to be conformed to the image of Christ as He promised (Rom. 8:29). And they fail under the description of the God-man's attributes. God's laws to them are written in stone, not on their hearts.

According to Paul, this Christian experience reverts to the slavery of the Old Covenant wrought at Sinai. The Old Covenant was a bilateral conditional agreement between God and man: if you obey My laws, I will bless you, and if you do not obey My commandments, I will curse you (Deut. 11:26-28). The demand was for humanity to use their best efforts to obey

God's laws to receive God's blessings. In Galatians, this effort is called the "works of the flesh."

(My book *One Truth* has two chapters in which the Old and New Covenant are contrasted.)

Whatever humanity can perform to fulfill God's laws and be like Jesus is destined for failure, as proven by 1500 years of Israel's failure to live by God's commandments. Just like Israel of old, Christians attempting to please God according to law struggle to control their actions while ignoring the Spirit's desire to transform their heart and nature from within. Consequently, they become discouraged and question God's promises. Therefore, the Christians' experience of forcing themselves to follow the law becomes burdensome, joyless slavery.

In Galatians 2:12, Paul says that these Jewish believers who were of the party of circumcision came from James and Jerusalem. They wanted to continue with the law of Moses to become righteous before God. In Galatians 4, Paul asserts that Hagar is equated to slavery under the law and the Jerusalem of their day: "Now Hagar is Mount Sinai in Arabia; she corresponds to the *present* Jerusalem, for she is in slavery with her children." (Galatians 4:25). What a shock that must have been to the Judaizers. Historically, the Jews have considered that Ishmael through Hagar as illegitimate, and his descendants have been consistent enemies of Israel ever since.

These Jewish Christians who are still under "Sinai" — the law of Moses — are openly told they are illegitimate in God's New Testament Covenant. They are enemies of God's people in the one Body of Christ. This revelation should expose and devastate the Judaizers and cause them to repent from the old to the new. Simultaneously, this should persuade all believers (both Gentiles and innocent Jewish believers) not to be distracted by the Judaizers' enticing words (although it "sounds so scriptural").

Circumcision Was a Type of the Crucified Christ

Due to Abraham's failure to produce an heir by his own effort (flesh), God came back in Genesis 17 to make the covenant[6] of circumcision. God repeated His promise: Abraham and all his descendants were to be circumcised.

---

6   The Abrahamic Covenant was unilateral, whereas the Old/First Covenant of Sinai (Moses) was bilateral. In other words, the Abrahamic Covenant was unconditionally kept by God's unfailing promise of the Seed. Whereas the Old Mosaic Covenant was utterly conditional: "if you will, then I will.")

As we have already pointed out previously, this act of circumcision was a precursor or type of Christ's work on the cross to terminate the flesh.

Circumcision was a painful reminder to Abraham that his work of the flesh was unacceptable and rejected by God. Since Abraham used his own efforts through his flesh to produce a son, God came to literally and physically cut off his flesh. Not only this, but Ishmael historically became a hindrance to Israel's journey over the centuries.

God promised Abraham He would have a seed who would inherit the good land of Canaan. The crucified and indwelling Christ fulfilled this promise by producing one Body, His ekklesia, among diverse people. This seed is the promised Seed (Gal. 3:29): a corporate Seed produced through grace. "Now you, brothers and sisters, like Isaac, are children of promise" (Gal. 4:28).

Paul called Hagar "Mount Sinai" (Gal. 4:24), which is the Old Covenant (or "first covenant" – Heb. 8:6-13) in slavery under the law. He equated Sarah to the free woman, which is the New Covenant enjoying the promise of grace. The law which is Mount Sinai was used to divide believers in the New Covenant. Meanwhile, the promised Seed fulfilled in the New Covenant is one corporate Seed enjoying grace. Therefore, any dividing of the Lord's Body is equated to a slave persecuting those enjoying grace (Gal. 4:29).

> "Those people [of the circumcision] are zealous to win you over, but for no good. What they want is to **alienate** you from us, so that you may have zeal for them."
>
> –Gal. 4:17, NIV

Abraham was struggling and doubting God's promise in Genesis 16. Therefore, God coming to him after thirteen years in Genesis 17 was a real encouragement to Abraham. This encouragement came with a mark of circumcision. Then centuries later, believers used this mark to alienate one group from another.

How Can God's Gifts Divide the Body of Christ?

Let's consider how God encouraging believers by providing helpful favor, enlightenment from Scripture, or a spiritual gift can be used to divide and separate God's people. For most Christians, during the initial period after coming to faith, they experience joy, victory, and an openness to share their testimony. They simply love Jesus and fellowship with other believers — no matter which church they attend. However, after a while, they begin experiencing struggles maintaining victory in their lives. These Christians become disappointed with their spiritual progress and start searching for answers concerning what can deliver them from failures and live the overcoming life. They may find something especially beneficial through seeking and prayer either directly from God, a scriptural passage, a minister, or a church. They experience a spiritual renewal in what some consider a "second visitation" from God. Some Christians call this the "second blessing," believing they will no longer be as tempted by sin and have achieved complete deliverance. Once again, the Christian life is exciting, and they find themselves victorious.

These spiritually helpful experiences or revelations take many forms. For some, it is a revelation to understand a doctrine from Scriptures such as justification by faith or eternal security of their salvation (once-saved-always-saved). Others may be inspired by a spiritual gift such as speaking in tongues, supernatural healing, or deliverance. Others find a church with a method of holiness and prayer that strengthens them to live in sanctification. In any case, those who have received such help, which has strengthened their Christian walk, now appreciate these instruments or gifts God used to empower them. However, instead of only giving credit and glory to God for this help, they credit their transformation to a specific tool God used.

Since it was a doctrine, gift, special prayer, minister, or method of holiness that empowered them, these would now be considered extraordinary. This believer lifts up the instrument which God used to enliven such a seeker. He preaches it so that others may receive help as he did. His enthusiasm for this instrument becomes his identity or brand. Naturally, this person finds comfort and support with a Christian group holding a similar doctrinal understanding or experience. A loyalty between him and this brand of Christianity develops; whereby, he desires to increase its adherence or defend it when challenged. Therefore, the very gracious visitation from God to strengthen this believer unwittingly becomes a mark dividing this person from others who did not receive help through the same instrument.

Some may say: "How can you not believe in once-saved-always-saved and instead believe that you can lose your salvation? You are preaching 'another gospel'!" Or they may say: "What, you do not speak in tongues?

You are really missing out on the Spirit." Haven't you heard something similar from Christians? These are examples that "circumcision" believers have used for centuries to divide from each other.

According to Paul in 1 Corinthians 1:12, even "I am of Jesus Christ" was a brand used to divide from other believers who identified themselves with Paul, Apollos, or Cephas. If Jesus Christ can become a brand to divide, in that case, it is not surprising that some who have been tremendously helped by the revelation of "loving one another" and the "oneness of the Body of Christ" can brand themselves with a "love" or "oneness" identity. While holding to this identity, they demean and separate from those they perceive as being "still under the law" (instead of love) or from those who are members of institutional churches (therefore "in division").

This kind of visitation can be experienced multiple times in a Christian's journey. If a believer does not learn that faith is enough to continue their journey and give glory only to God in Jesus Christ, then each time, they will proclaim another instrument God used in their life. They bounce from one brand to another, all the while alienating themselves from other Christians bearing a mark different from theirs.

Understanding how the Judaizers used "circumcision" to divide and separate from the uncircumcised, makes it clear Galatians is apropos for today — by helping believers in the present state of increasing divisions, alienation, and sectarianism. We can learn a lot from Galatians bringing God's people into one fellowship in the Lord's one Body.

5

FREEDOM AND THE FRUIT OF THE SPIRIT

The Sons Are Free

> For in Christ Jesus you are all sons of God, through faith.
>
> –Gal 3:26
>
> But when the fullness of time had come, God sent forth his Son, born of woman, born under the law, to redeem those who were under the law, so that we might receive adoption as sons. And because you are sons, God has sent the Spirit of his Son into our hearts, crying, "Abba! Father!" So you are no longer a slave, but a son, and if a son, then an heir through God.
>
> –Gal 4:4-7

It is truly extraordinary that men (male and female) can become sons of God. The word for sons (*huios*) here in Greek is the same word identifying Jesus as the Son of God in verses 4 and 6. Of course, believers are not in the Godhead as the Son of God; however, they have the same divine life and nature as Jesus Christ, the Son. Jesus, in relation to the Godhead, is the Only Begotten Son, and in relation to His followers, He is the Firstborn among many brothers (Rom. 8:29). Believers have the same life and nature as Christ which enables them to be called into the *fellowship* eternally existing between the Father and the Son (*koinonia* – "partaker" of the "divine nature" – 2 Peter 1:4).

Additionally, there was no price to pay nor work done to earn being a son of God. Human beings become sons of God simply through faith. This is confirmed in John 1:12, "But to all who did receive him, who believed in his name, he gave the right to become children of God." Christians are born of God by simply believing into Jesus Christ. It is through the hearing of faith a person is born of God.

Due to the fall of man into sin, man came under the curse of the law. In fact, the more mankind works to fulfill the law, the more they experience the curse of the law (Gal. 3:10). Christ's death was to redeem man from the law and its curse. However, the Judaizers did their best to bring the Gentile believers back to the law and under slavery. Therefore, Paul had to declare to the Gentile believers that they are now sons of God and no longer need the law as a guardian (Gal. 3:24).

This phrase "adoption as sons" is from a compound Greek word (*huiothesia*) composed of a son, an offspring, and "a placing" (Vine's). Therefore, believers are truly sons born of God the Father versus just being adopted without blood or genetic relationships. God didn't adopt man like one adopts a pet dog. The word *huiothesia* highlights that these believers who were once outside of God now have a legal place as God's sons. Rather than contradicting the fact of a birth relationship, this word emphasizes the switch from being a person with a fallen nature to having the divine nature and eternal life of God.

Believers know they are sons because they have the Spirit of God's Son in their hearts, and they cry out "Abba! Father!" This same address of "Abba Father" was used by Jesus Christ when He called out to the Father during the most vulnerable point of His life on earth when He contemplated going to the cross (Mark 14:36). "Abba" is the word a son uses to express warm affection to his father.[7] Since believers have the Spirit of His Son through a real birth from God the Father, they also have the same relationship with God as their Father as Jesus Christ has with the Father. Therefore, they cry out "Abba Father" in the same warmth, love, and affection as Jesus.

The Jews believed their relationship with God as their Father was unique to them (Isa. 63:16). However, Paul refers to the Judaizers as those under slavery, whereas all those, both Jews and Gentiles, through faith are sons. Through faith, they both now have the same Father and should both cry out, "Abba Father!" to be in the same sweet fellowship with the Father.

Sons are no longer under the law under slavery. The sons are free. As soon as there is a temptation to cut off another believer from fellowship, immediately there should be a cry of "Abba Father!" to stay in the warm embrace of the Father. It is in the fellowship of the Father believers can be true brothers and sisters loving each other with the love of the Father. Crying "Abba Father!" keeps believers in the loving relationship

---

7   https://www.biblestudytools.com/dictionaries/eastons-bible-dictionary/abba.html

between the Father and the sons, and it is in this love that all conflicts are solved peacefully.

Freedom from Both Circumcision and Uncircumcision

> For freedom Christ has set us free; stand firm therefore, and do not submit again to a yoke of slavery . . .. I testify again to every man who accepts circumcision that he is obligated to keep the whole law. You are severed from Christ, you who would be justified by the law; you have fallen away from grace . . . . For in Christ Jesus neither circumcision nor uncircumcision counts for anything, but only faith working through love.
>
> –Gal 5:1, 3-4, 6

Paul clearly states circumcision or uncircumcision doesn't count for anything. One is not superior or more blessed than the other. Believers can be different in every way, but the way of faith with which they entered and remain in Christ is the same — that is their commonality of oneness. In Christ Jesus, all the distinctions do not separate because every person was transferred into Christ by faith working through love.

Even though circumcision is nothing, it was an identity and branding of those under law. To the Judaizers, it was a sign of being under the law of Moses. To Christians today, their mark of "circumcision" is under the "law" of their church brand. Paul condemned the Judaizers' zeal for recruiting and converting Christians to their Jewish brand of circumcision (Gal. 4:17).

In their experience, those Christians striving to be righteous according to any brand of law sever themselves from Christ. They sever themselves from what Christ has accomplished on the cross to break down the middle wall of partition between contrary or differentiated believers. Additionally, they sever from the corporate Body of Christ. Those divided by their "circumcision" are severed from the greater fellowship in the Body of Christ.

Some Christians pride themselves in being "uncircumcised" — not under the law. They bear a mark of "uncircumcision" in their factiousness. They may consider themselves to be "progressive" or "liberal" Christians and view those under the law to be "conservative" or "legalistic" Christians. With their freedom from being under the law, these *progressive* Christians can become equally divisive, separating themselves from the law-oriented/keeping conservatives. Therefore, both circumcision and uncircumcision are meaningless in Christ since both can divide and keep believers from being experientially one in Him.

Every believer has been set free. This freedom is in Christ. They are free to fellowship with God's diverse people no matter how different they are from each other. This freedom was immediate at the time of faith in Jesus Christ. The love toward all of God's people was instantaneous and unconditional. Their mark of freedom was their love for all the brethren, whether circumcised or uncircumcised, since they had passed from death into life (1 John 3:14).

Freedom to Love One Another

> For you were called to freedom, brothers. Only do not use your freedom as an opportunity for the flesh, but through love serve one another. For the whole law is fulfilled in one word: "You shall love your neighbor as yourself."
>
> −Gal 5:13-14

The freedom believers have received in Christ is not a license to sin. No, just because they are not under the law doesn't mean they can steal, cheat, get drunk, or live in sexual immorality. That is not the purpose of being freed from the law.

Having freedom from the law is to serve one another through love. Jewish believers in Galatians 2 didn't love Gentile believers due to the law's requirements that they should not eat with uncircumcised sinners (Acts 10:28). Being under the law makes one selective regarding which Christians they care for and serve. To be free from the law is to have the ability to serve every believer, including those holding views contrary to one's perspective. This supports the idea that the law described in Galatians did not focus on morality. Christians are free from every law dividing them to serve one another as Jesus served them.

Coming back again to these Jewish believers in Galatians 2: because they were under the law, they couldn't fellowship with their Gentile counterparts (both were believers in Christ). Indeed, that is not loving your neighbor as yourself: they were eating and fellowshipping with their Gentile neighbors, but the law came with the circumcision party — they separated because love was gone. If these Jewish believers wanted to fulfill the law, they would have loved their Gentile neighbors — since loving your neighbor is the actual fulfillment of the "whole law."

Some Christians suggest that though they divide from other believers by not having fellowship, they still love them. This would amount to love in words, but "not in deed" (1 John 3:18). Consider this: the God Who is love came in the Son to die solving the problem of sin and separation. His sacrifice resulted in fellowship, intimate sharing, and communion of the Holy Spirit with those for whom He died. God's definition of love leads to one fellowship and community of the Holy Spirit. Therefore, it is dishonest to claim love for someone you have fenced off and with whom you refuse to have fellowship.

Let's define a neighbor as anyone in close proximity of a relationship, whether close to your home, students in the same classes or dorm, colleagues at work, or relatives. Believers should actively seek fellowship with other Christians with contrary views in their "neighborhood" and love them. Believers do not need to agree with each other since our ultimate agreement is Christ Himself:

- A Protestant should reach out to a Catholic and vice-versa.
- A Pentecostal should reach out to reformed believers and vice-versa.
- A democrat should reach out to a republican and vice-versa.
- A pro-life should reach out to the pro-choice and vice-versa.
- An anti-vaxxer should reach out to the pro-vaxxer and vice-versa.

Since Christians have so many divisions and factions, how many differing believers we can reach out and love in our vicinity is virtually endless.

Live in and by the Power of the Spirit

> But I say, walk by the Spirit, and you will not gratify the desires of the flesh. For the desires of the flesh are against the Spirit, and the desires of the Spirit are against the flesh, for these are opposed to each other, to keep you from doing the things you want to do. But if you are led by the Spirit, you are not under the law.
>
> —Gal 5:16-18

In contrast to living by the law, using the efforts of the flesh, here Paul charges believers to walk or live in the realm of the Spirit and by the power of the Spirit. Some translations use "walk in the Spirit," and others say "walk by the Spirit." It could be both: Believers are in the sphere of the Spirit and are empowered by the Spirit. The "walk" here in the Greek means to be in that state: *wherever you are, where you go, live and walk at large in the state of the Spirit.* This is living in the good land of Christ, the Spirit.

In the Old Covenant, the people of Israel only had their own strength to keep God's laws: YOU shall love your God . . . YOU shall love your neighbor (Matt. 22:36-40). It all depends on YOU (again, a bilateral contract). However, in the New Covenant, Jesus Christ lives in His followers (Gal. 2:20). Jesus is both in His believers and in the heavens since He is also the Spirit. He is no longer merely physical. He is also the life-giving Spirit (1 Cor. 15:45). What a mystery! How wonderful that God the Father, God the Son, and God the Holy Spirit are all included in the Spirit.

When God created man (male and female), he created man with three parts: body, soul, and spirit (1 Thess. 5:23). The human spirit within man was reserved for receiving, containing, and fellowshipping with God. But due to sin, man's spirit was deadened and severed from God. However, man's spirit still has the potential of the new birth by the Spirit of God. Not only that, but the Spirit is joined to the human spirit of all His believers. Therefore, Christ's crucifixion and resurrection not only washed away all the penalty wrought by our sins (i.e., death) but also made it possible for man's spirit to become enlivened by receiving the Spirit through faith (John 3:6; Eph. 2:5; Gal. 3:2).

The Old Covenant law was external, demanding man use his strength of the flesh to follow and obey. However, the New Covenant is God's life and nature coming into man, joining Himself, and becoming one Spirit in man

(1 Cor. 6:17) so that God's nature would become the law of life within man (Jer. 31:33; Ezek. 36:26-27; Rom. 8:2). It is full participation or *koinonia*/ fellowship with His divine nature (2 Pet. 1:4). Believers are not doing this independently but in "fellowship" with the Living God! Fulfilling God's law is not by man's works of the flesh. It is the natural working and expression of Jesus Christ living in man — God's life in union with humanity.

Paul's charge: Forget about trying to fulfill God's law by the works of your flesh. Focus on the Spirit within. Walk and enjoy the love and grace of the Trinity, and you will naturally bear the image of Christ. Be in constant fellowship in the Holy Spirit wherever you go or in whatever you do. Don't be discouraged when you succumb to temptation and fall into sin. Instead, repent immediately — turn back to Jesus, praise Him for His precious blood, enjoy the righteousness before God through faith, and continue to fellowship in His love and grace.

Obviously, believers should do their best to abide by the laws of human society to avoid the penalty of prison or fines. However, like the Old Covenant, the laws of society aim to control people's actions or behaviors, but such laws cannot change their human nature.

(My book *One Life & Glory* dives into the details of living, enjoying, and growing in and by the Spirit.)

The Results of the Works of the Flesh

Now the works of the flesh are obvious: sexual immorality, moral impurity, promiscuity, idolatry, sorcery, hatreds, strife, jealousy, outbursts of anger, selfish ambitions, dissensions, factions, envy, drunkenness, carousing, and anything similar. I am warning you about these things — as I warned you before — that those who practice such things will not inherit the kingdom of God.

–Gal 5:19-21

It is counter-intuitive that those who try to fulfill the law using the works of the flesh end up with a long list of negative characteristics. This situation is similar to what Paul said in Romans 7: While he tries to do good, evil is present. The result: what he should do according to God's law, he doesn't, and what he shouldn't do, he does. In fact, when he tries not to covet by his own effort, he covets even more. Since sin is in the flesh (fallen) nature, we can conclude that there are damaging and destructive side effects when we attempt to use the flesh to do the good.

Usually, when Christians cite the "works of the flesh," they will point out the obvious items such as sexual immorality, sorcery, idolatry, drunkenness, or anger. However, this list includes selfish ambition, dissensions (divisions), envy, and factions. The first list consists of those actions affecting a person's physical well-being and holiness. The second list has to do with relationships with others. Nevertheless, the latter list of items is typically considered acceptable and even normal among Christians.

Let's consider "selfish ambitions" among Christians. The Greek word, according to Vine's Expository Dictionary means "being ambitious to win followers." Generally, each church or ministry is ambitious to grow its adherents. The word for "dissension" above is a word describing a more pronounced division: "*dichostasia*" means "a standing apart" (Vine's). It is common to see this definition applied among Christians in various churches. Christians identified with one church may not fellowship with other believers outside their group because they "stand apart" from those who do not share the same convictions or perspectives as their church. Even within the same church, there can be cliques which stand apart from each other.

Paul in Romans 16:17 charged believers to mark those ministers who caused "*dichostasia*" or divisions since they were causing believers to stand apart and not receive greetings (fellowship) from other Christians. These ministers only cared about growing their own groups to serve their bellies instead of increasing the fellowship in the one Body of Christ. Generally, we don't think such ministers causing divisions are doing the works of the flesh since they are preaching the gospel (though with distortion), teaching the Bible, or promoting some form of holiness. Nevertheless, these practices are works of the flesh.

Finally, there are *factions*, which is "*hairesis*" in the Greek. This word was anglicized in KJV to be "heresy." *Heresy* in the mind of most Christians conjures up false or unorthodox teachings concerning the person and work of Jesus Christ. However, the accurate meaning of this word is making a choice or a sect (Vine's). Therefore, "*hairesis*" is when there is a dispute between two groups with opposing points of views, and a person is now put in a position to make a choice as to which group he or she belongs. If so, then both opposing groups are sects (factions), since each member of both groups made a choice. The members bear the brand of the group of their choice. A member of one faction typically does not fellowship with members in the other faction due to disputes between the groups and each accusing the other group of error.

Additionally, within these factions there are those who are zealous, and their zealousness becomes an agenda; whereby, they would force believers into an uncomfortable position to make a choice: are you for or opposed to our group's perspectives, doctrines, experiences, giftings, or whatever it may be. Their goal is to grow their faction by converting more Christians to their way of thinking. This may be the final step of separation starting from selfish ambition, becoming divisive, and resulting in factiousness.

We can ascribe all three of the above characteristics to these Jewish believers in Galatians 2. Those Judaizers of the circumcision party, who came from James (Gal. 2:12), certainly had a selfish ambition to grow their group. Peter then took the lead to stand apart from these Gentile believers. Subsequently, the other Jewish believers choose to follow and be in the sect or faction of the circumcised, thereby alienating themselves from ethnic believers of Christ's ekklesia called out from among the nations. Additionally, individual Gentile believers are put into an uncomfortable (literally painful) position: whether or not to be circumcised to join these Jewish believers.

Oh, how Satan has deceived Christians! Around the globe Christians generally will point out drunkenness, fornications, idol worship, orgies, or outbursts of anger as sins of the flesh and universally condemn them. However, selfish ambitions, divisions, and factions that have caused increasing separation or alienation among Christians are generally accepted as the norm in Christianity.

According to Paul, those practicing any of "the works of the flesh" will "not inherit the kingdom of God." Some claim they are for "the Kingdom of God" and its manifestation — they proudly identify themselves as "kingdom people" who are "disciples of the King." Yet "inheriting the kingdom of God" has everything to do with these issues of division and alienation in the Body of Christ. So, while Christians do their best to overcome one set of obvious sins, they are ignorantly and happily practicing another category.

Christians may even pray, seeking deliverance from the first category since it could be damaging their health and holiness. Deliverance from any sin is undoubtedly excellent and commendable. However, while seeking such deliverance, they may practice the second category of these "sins of the flesh": those that destroy the Body of Christ's oneness, fellowship, and testimony. Many groups that have helped believers overcome the first category have become groups in the second category throughout history. Satan still wins because these are also works of the flesh keeping people out of the kingdom of God.

The Fruit of the Spirit

> But the fruit of the Spirit is love, joy, peace, patience, kindness, goodness, faithfulness, gentleness, self-control; against such things there is no law.
>
> –Gal 5:22-23

Believers who continue to receive the supply of the Spirit by faith (Gal. 3:5), those receiving the promised seed through the free woman (Gal. 4:21-31), those walking and living in and by the Spirit (Gal 5:16), they are the ones who bear the fruit of the Spirit. It is a singular fruit, not fruits (plural) of the Spirit. One fruit contains all the attributes of the Spirit. Similar to one God with Father, Son, and Spirit, here in one fruit is love, joy, peace, patience, kindness, and all the rest.

Some Christians pray specifically for one or a few of these items. They say, "What I need is more joy and peace," but these items are not for one to pick and choose. Contained within this one fruit of the Spirit is everything they need for themselves and their relationship with others. You can't be selfish with this fruit by only seeking an attribute just for yourself. You will have something for yourself if you care for your relationship with others. For example, you can have joy and peace by yourself: between you and God. However, love, patience, kindness, and gentleness require a community of people to experience. Only in a community with dissimilar, antagonistic, and challenging people will the fruit (love, patience, kindness, and gentleness) shine forth and manifest.

Fruit is the product of life and nature. In fact, reproduction is a clear definition of life. Every life, including God's life, reproduces or "bears fruit." This new life in believers started when God planted the divine seed at the time of faith in Jesus Christ through His Word (1 Pet. 1:23). Humanity is the "dirt" in which the Seed of God was sown. Just about all seeds seem insignificant: tiny without much outward appeal; however, these seeds grow and bear fruit after being planted in soil. The fruit is the result of the reproduction and multiplication of the seed mingled with the dirt. The fruit is the beauty and expansion of the seed plus the minerals in the soil; what's more, this fruit is nourishing for food.

Many Christians believe the fruit of the Spirit must be a supernatural or miraculous work and manifestation. However, the fruit of the Spirit, as described in Galatians 5, is very human. Humanity (the dirt) is necessary to bear this fruit. Not one of these items (love, joy, peace, patience, kindness, goodness, faithfulness, gentleness, self-control) in the fruit of the Spirit is inherently supernatural. Every human being can claim these characteristics at one time or another.

How Is the Spirit Expressed and Manifested in Virtues Which Are so Ordinary?

When one's natural ability runs out, and these characteristics of the fruit of the Spirit continue to flourish, the Spirit is manifested. For example, people who are not enjoying the supply of the Spirit at a certain point or situation will run out of patience and endurance. Others may find themselves unable to forgive the same offenses from a person. Still, others may find some people simply unlovable. When these things happen, those finding their supply in the Spirit will continue beyond what others expect of them. Those observing will be mystified how a believer can continue having patience under unbearably demanding circumstances, or how another believer can love and care for an enemy, or how a Christian can extend forgiveness to those who keep offending unreasonably.

Fruit is the natural and predictable outcome of life. We do not have to guess what kind of fruit will result from planting an apple seed. It is impossible to see a mango fruit from an orange seed. A dog will always bear puppies and not kittens. A human mother does not have to pray to God and hope her baby is not a monkey. In the same way, the Spirit will predictably bear His fruit in humanity. No prayer for miracles is needed. Instead, believers can simply continue to enjoy and grow in God's eternal-divine life and in time fruit will automatically manifest, according to His schedule.

(My book, *One Life & Glory* contains *four* essentials, whereby all believers need *to* grow and mature spontaneously.)

Galatians

6

BEAR ONE
ANOTHER'S BURDENS

Restoring a Transgressor

> Brothers, if anyone is caught in any transgression, you who
> are spiritual should restore him in a spirit of gentleness. Keep
> watch on yourself, lest you too be tempted. Bear one another's
> burdens, and so fulfill the law of Christ. For if anyone thinks he
> is something, when he is nothing, he deceives himself.
>
> ~Gal 6:1-3

In the final chapter, Paul continues his dialogue with the negative pattern of the separation of the Jewish believers in Galatians 2 in view. Galatians 5-6 are Paul's "pragmatics" when it comes to living by the "truth of the gospel." Believers are to care for each other, bear each other's burdens, and shouldn't think of themselves as better than others. Indeed, these Jewish believers thought that these other ethnic peoples (Gentiles) were transgressors of the law (sinners). That was the reason they separated themselves from these Gentile Christians. Even if these Gentiles were sinners, Jewish believers should not divide but should have stayed with these transgressors and restored fellowship with them in a spirit of gentleness.

Christians are often very harsh in their judgment of each other. They often consider unbelievers are ignorant and need the gospel, but those professing Christ should know better. One type of Christian may judge another believer strictly. They separate from transgressors who have fallen into the sins of the body, such as drunkenness or sexual immorality. Another type of believer is harsh toward those who commit doctrinal transgressions or variance in worship or Christian practices.

A person who thinks that he is something would have the arrogance to judge others. Such a person may consider it beneath them to stoop down to bear a transgressor's burden. They would not want to soil their holiness. Therefore, if anyone thinks he is something, he deceives himself. Paul's point is that everyone is nothing. No matter who he is and what he may have accomplished, he is nothing. If anyone thinks otherwise, he is deceived.

Paul was probably the greatest apostle, but he said he is the "least of all saints" (Eph. 3:8). Near the end of his ministry, he still identified himself as "the chief sinner" (1 Tim. 1:15). He was not faking humility; he was serving in that reality. He followed the pattern of Jesus when He told His disciples to lower themselves to be a slave and wash each other's feet. Paul never thought that he was something; therefore, he could be all things to all men in order to serve them and bear them to Christ (1 Cor. 9:19).

Whichever the sin may be, if they determine that another believer is a transgressor, Paul tells us to "restore such a one" (Gal. 6:1-2). This ability to restore by bearing the burden of a transgressor is a manifestation of "I am crucified with Christ" and "Christ lives in me." The "I" who thinks that he is "something" is crucified, and the one living is the Servant of all, the Bearer of all burdens.

Restoration is not possible without fellowship expressed through love. When approaching such individuals who were labeled transgressors, Paul tells us to approach them with gentleness, not condemnation or condescension. We should be careful not to be conceited with a holier-than-thou attitude. Instead, extend a hand of fellowship to supply and support the so-called "transgressors." One day, the role may reverse itself when the transgressor becomes the restorer.

In Galatians 5:14, loving your neighbor as yourself fulfills the law of God. Fulfilling the law of Christ looks like bearing one another's burdens and bearing another's burden is the practical manifestation of love. In Matthew 11:28-30, Jesus said to ". . . come to me, all who are heavy laden" and "take my yoke . . . my burden is light." They need to come to Him to take on Jesus' yoke and bear the burden together. Bearing His yoke and His burden together is impossible without being with Jesus.

How do we bear one another's burdens? Jesus' words show it is essential to come together and be yoked together. Believers need to be yoked together to bear one another's burdens. These Jewish believers did the opposite by unyoking themselves from their Gentile Christian counterparts in Antioch.

They broke the law by trying to keep the law. Therefore, Paul encouraged them to return and be re-yoked with these Gentile believers to fulfill the law.

Consider how Christians have rejected each other over the many diverse "transgressions" they have assessed on each other. Jesus was willing to be yoked with every sinner who was dissimilar to Him so that He could bear their burdens while they bear His. Therefore, believers are to do the same with each other. We are not just bearing each other's burden, but also the Lord's burden, which includes His burden for the building up His Body: The Ekklesia.

Many churches/ministries have used Matthew 18:17 to say that if a believer has transgressed and refuses to hear the "church" in repentance, they should be treated as a tax collector and sinner. These ministries teach their members they should no longer welcome such a one into fellowship, saying they should avoid this sinner (cut off from fellowship). Many churches use this method as a threat for disciplining their members.

Creating such an application is an overreach and an abuse of the verse's original context. Furthermore, it is inconsistent with Jesus' example. Let's say that someone has indeed transgressed and refused to hear the "church" for repentance, and they are now considered equal to a tax collector and sinner. Didn't Jesus eat and drink with tax collectors and sinners? That means Jesus continued to have fellowship by bearing this unrepentant sinner's burden. He has not given up on healing this sinner. If that is the case, why should believers with Jesus living in them cut off communication or fellowship with such a person who refuses to hear the "church"?

However, Ekklesia is a privilege where every believer has the right to participate freely; therefore, there are conditions in which a believer forfeits this privilege of participation until reconciliation occurs. The following would disqualify a believer from participation in an assembly of the Lord's Ekklesia: one who has an agenda to cause divisions in the Body (Rom. 16:17-18; Titus 3:9-10); one who lives openly, shamelessly boasting of their sinful life (1 Cor. 5:1-11); one who falsely teaches that Jesus is not God who came in the flesh (2 John 1:7-11); and one who is capable to work, but does not work thereby becoming a busybody to cause trouble (2 Thess. 3:6-15). (See chapter 11 of One Ekklesia by this author for a more thorough discussion of exclusion from the Ekklesia).

Sows to the Flesh or to the Spirit

> Do not be deceived: God is not mocked, for whatever one sows, that will he also reap. For the one who sows to his own flesh will from the flesh reap corruption, but the one who sows to the Spirit will from the Spirit reap eternal life.
>
> –Gal 6:7-8

It doesn't take a revelation to understand that a person's sins such as drunkenness, sexual immorality, stealing, or extortion are sowing to the flesh, which will reap corruption. Even non-Christians can recognize that these sins are bad for health, peace-of-mind, and can even land a person in prison. However, in context through the entire letter, Paul's focus was not on such immoralities. His definition of sowing to the flesh was counterintuitive: being righteous according to law, using fleshly energy to fulfill the law, or bearing a "mark of righteousness" (e.g., circumcision), thus alienating other believers. Therefore, the reaping of corruption makes one become a slave, lose grace, and divide the Body of Christ.

According to Galatians, here is how a believer sows to the Spirit:

- Don't divide from believers who hold views contrary to yours (Gal 2:12)
- Live by faith to be righteous before God (Gal 3:11)
- Remain in the death of Christ so as not to use fleshly energy to fulfill God's law (Gal. 2:20, 3:2-3)
- Enjoy the grace in others since Christ lives in them (Gal. 2:20-21)
- Walk daily in and by the Spirit (Gal. 5:25)
- Restore the transgressors (Gal. 6:1)
- Bear each other's burdens, sharing good things with those who teach (Gal. 6:2, 6)
- Do good to all, especially those in the household of faith (Gal. 6:9-10)

Since Paul was writing to believers, eternal life here doesn't refer to the future coming kingdom where all God's people are written in the book of life. Paul wanted his readers to see believers sowing to the Spirit can reap eternal life today. Reaping eternal life today undoubtedly includes the fruit of the Spirit: where believers are no longer under the law and are therefore free to fellowship with all other believers. It was the illegitimate use of the law which divided Jewish believers from Gentile believers. Therefore, Paul emphasized there is no law against the fruit of the Spirit (Gal. 5:23).

Psalm 133 says: "How good and pleasant it is for brethren to dwell together in unity . . . for there the Lord commanded the blessing of eternal life." Just as the psalmist declared God's blessings of eternal life upon those in unity, the reaping of eternal life in Galatians 6:8 is due to sowing to the Spirit by keeping the unity of the Body. How joyful and blessed are those sowing to the Spirit and reaping eternal life! They will stay yoked together and in fellowship with each other for the Lord's Ekklesia, no matter how divergent they are from each other. They will not separate from each other even if they bear different marks of "circumcision" or not "circumcised" at all.

Converting Other Believers to Your Brand

> It is those who want to make a good showing in the flesh who would force you to be circumcised, and only in order that they may **not** be persecuted for the cross of Christ. For even those who are circumcised do not themselves keep the law, but they desire to have you circumcised that they may boast in your flesh.
>
> ~Gal 6:12-13

At the end of Paul's letter, his attention was back to "circumcision." Paul undoubtedly uses this word to remind his readers of the situation in Galatians 2 when Peter separated from the Gentiles. It was the "circumcision party" from James (Jerusalem) which struck fear in the apostle Peter causing him (and Barnabas) and all Jewish believers who were present to separate from the Gentiles in Antioch. How powerful and fearsome the circumcision party must have been to terrorize the great and fearless Peter! This same Peter who preached at Pentecost to thousands and suffered much persecution. Their actions caused Peter to extinguish (functionally) God's eternal purpose: His Ekklesia. Exposing this division was Paul's driving motivation for writing this epistle by defending the truth of the gospel.

The Judaizers wanted to gain more converts to circumcision by basically "forcing" these Gentile believers to be circumcised — to come under the law of Moses. Although they didn't physically force Gentiles to be circumcised, they hoped that by separating and dividing from the Gentiles these Gentile Christians would be shamed into circumcision by a fear of rejection.

By standing firm in their Jewish Christian faction, the Gentiles who were new to the ways of Yahweh and His Son, Jesus Christ, would be attracted to conversion (circumcision) thus becoming like the Jews. At that time, those of the party of the circumcision had the reputation for being God's people. It was a difficult proposition for Gentile believers to refute that Peter, Barnabas, James (the brother of Jesus), and those at Pentecost should be knowledgeable and be a pattern for all Gentile Christians.

These Judaizers were believers in Christ as the Lamb of God Who took away their sins on the Cross. They believed Jesus to be the Messiah executing God's will of bringing back God's kingdom. However, they lacked the revelation that the cross of Christ was to break down the middle wall between Jews and Gentiles creating "in Himself one new man" (Eph. 2:15). They were also unable to see that the kingdom of God consists of people from every tribe, tongue, nation, and people (Rev. 5:9-10).

Being alienated from Gentile Christians allowed Jewish believers to escape persecution from those in their Jewish Christian community. The word "persecute" in Greek means to drive away or put to flight (*BLB Outline of Biblical Usage*). The motivation for escaping persecution or not being driven away from the Jewish Christian community was so strong that even Peter and Barnabas collapsed in fear and divided from their Gentile counterparts. The Judaizers did not fully understand the Cross. They would not be persecuted for believing in the Cross taking away the sins of the world; however, they would be persecuted by their Jewish faction (let alone the Jewish nation) if they joined in fellowship with Gentile believers. Yet, this union between Jew and Gentile was what the cross of Christ intended and accomplished! It is difficult for us today to come to grips as to the chasm which existed between Jew and Gentile during the early days of His ekklesia in the first century.

In other words, the cross of Christ specifically accomplished the oneness of people by bringing them, who are divided and hostile to each other, into one new man (John 11:52; Eph. 2:14-17). Jewish believers who joined themselves in fellowship with Gentile believers are those walking according to the finished work of the cross. However, if they did, they would have been shunned by their Jewish Christian community (the "circumcision), persecuted (driven away) for the cross of Christ. Therefore, in order to be accepted and not persecuted, they separated from these Gentile believers, thereby maintaining their Jewish identity.

There was boasting by the Judaizers when they could convert a Gentile believer to become circumcised. Their goal was to convert Gentile Christians to bear the sign of righteousness according to law; therefore, everyone converted was a "win." Certainly any "win" deserves glory and rejoicing, that was their boasting. "Boasting in your flesh" has a double meaning: First, the Judaizers gloried when a Gentile literally cut off a piece of his flesh. Second, these "spiritual enemies" rejoiced when one could leave the simplicity of faith in Christ alone and commit himself to fulfilling the law by the flesh, using his own efforts and energy.

The goal of the Judaizer was not really to fulfill God's law since they knew they could not — no one can. Paul made it emphatically clear that no one could be justified or be righteous before God by working to fulfill the law (Rom. 3:20). Paul even called Peter and the rest of the Jewish believers *hypocrites*: acting righteously by separating from the Gentiles while breaking the law like the Gentiles. The Judaizer's motivation was not about perfecting or equipping the Gentiles in their Christian journey. Instead, it was all about gaining converts to their brand of Christianity, which separated them from other so-called "inferior" believers.

Christians throughout history have followed the example set by the Judaizers by using many things to divide believers: doctrinal understanding and interpretations, spiritual and supernatural gifts, methods of sanctification and appearances of holiness, the charisma of ministers, leadership styles and approaches, politics, socio-economic issues and social justice, race relations, life or choice, vax, or anti-vax. Factions have formed along any of these positions. Additionally, there is an explosion of divisions and factions by picking, choosing, and combining a growing menu of doctrinal perspectives and practices that create the ingredients for yet another new group.

In some circles, one cannot be identified simply by faith in Christ and peace with all believers in Him without declaring to which "faith community" they belong. Once "formal membership" is achieved, there are benefits associated with that alliance. Division is especially evident at the "communion table" when one does not meet the group's criterion (spoken or unspoken) then they are excluded from participation.

Consider how many combinations there are to form a community of believers: a charismatic Catholic group supporting pro-life is divided from a charismatic Evangelical group that is also pro-life. Both are divided from a Pentecostal group that is pro-choice, and all three may be divided from a black Pentecostal group supporting the BLM movement. What's more, they are all divided from another Pentecostal group teaching that holiness means women must wear long skirts with no make-up. Additionally, the charismatic groups mentioned above oppose another Pentecostal group that believes in once-saved-always-saved. The amalgamation for forming differentiated groups based on peculiar doctrines and practices, as well as style of worship or charismatic individuals is nearly endless.

All these divided groups can claim how Scriptures support their position as more enlightened, blessed, or orthodox than other groups. Many of these groups will have a brand or a mark to show their distinctions. Those more zealous in the groups are motivated to convert other Christians to their perspectives. Christians who lack strong convictions for either side may feel pressured to choose a side when faced with controversies between believers from opposing groups. Either way, by dividing, they miss the TRUTH of the gospel.

Believers who identify with one of these groups commonly feel compelled to spread their group's perspectives to other believers hoping others will convert to their brand of Christianity. There is a kind of glory and rejoicing when another Christian is added and becomes "circumcised" with their mark. Their preaching is unknowingly a distortion of the gospel since in their enthusiastic speaking concerning the enlightenment or orthodoxy which differentiates their group distracts believers to seek something other than the simple faith of Jesus Christ. Those who are zealous in promoting the blessings of their group are typically an integral part of a church community. Anyone in that community who fellowships with Christians holding an opposing view is frowned upon and often ostracized until they pull away from this person.[8] This, in essence, is persecution on behalf of the cross of Christ since all believers should have freedom of fellowship, especially with those who hold a contrary view for building up the one Body of Christ. Thus, Christians can become the Judaizers of today and should find the warning found in Galatians completely applicable.

---

8   There was but one meeting between the reformers, Martin Luther and Ulrich Zwingli, known as the Marburg Colloquy. They sought to settle their differences concerning the "Real Presence of Christ in the Eucharist." Both remained adamant in their convictions. Regardless of who was doctrinally right or wrong, the issue remained unresolved. When departing Zwingli asked Luther if they could at least consider themselves "brothers" Dr. Martin refused and said he would go only so far as "friends" but no further. Such are the rancorous differences which have divided believers in Christ for centuries.

First-century Jewish believers deserve sympathy and empathy from today's readers concerning their biases, distortion of the gospel, and factious actions. They inherited centuries of Judaism as described by the Hebrew Scriptures. According to the law and covenants, it was in their blood to feel superior over Gentiles because they were taught Gentiles were unclean dogs and sinners needing conversion. They didn't have the privilege of reading and studying Paul's epistles of Galatians, Romans, Corinthians, Ephesians, or Colossians. Although they had the Council in Jerusalem in Acts 15, the conclusion from James was so extraordinary that it is reasonable to forgive them for not getting it right the first time.

Even today, many Christian students and teachers haven't understood the explosive impact of James' conclusion. Case in point: Caiaphas, the high priest, prophesied in John 11 without really knowing what he was saying. Therefore, it is possible James, under the inspiration of the Spirit, made his paradigm-shifting judgment without fully comprehending the implications of what he decreed.

Christians today should not receive the same sympathy shown to the Judaizers because 27 New Testament books have circulated for almost 2000 years. Additionally, the printed Bible has been readily accessible for over 500 years. Believers have no excuse for not receiving the knowledge of the truth as recorded in the New Testament. The revelation of the work of Christ on the cross breaking down the wall of hatred between His divided people should be common knowledge. God's eternal purpose concerning His ekklesia should be the mission and goal of every minister of Christ.

The Lord's Ekklesia Is Not the Forum for Any Agendas

Churches today are owned by certain ministers or ministries. As such, every church has a unique emphasis on ministering to God's people. Every successful ministry, which can have its own church, must have helped God's people in some way. Here are a few examples of how churches help their people: scriptural teachings from a particular enlightened perspective, a technique for receiving and experiencing spiritual gifts, a method to strengthen Christians' holy living, deliverance from spiritual bondages, prosperity strategy, even catering to one specific language/ethnic group, or transparency in fellowship leading to in-depth discipleship. Various churches have genuinely helped multitudes of believers from around the globe. However, churches also have their brand of Christianity, which has divided God's people. The goal is not to reform churches since each ministry does God's work through different giftings and assignments. Churches as ministries are necessary since God has given a multitude of differing ministries (1 Cor. 12:4-5). However, they must recognize God's goal is not to build their church/ministry. Instead, His goal is to build His ekklesia: His Body.

This "differential" (ministry and ekklesia) is crucial. According to Paul, the gifted five-fold ministers are to equip the saints to build up the Body of Christ, so that all diverse saints might arrive at the unity of the faith: "the fullness of Christ" (Eph. 4:11-13). Without the end goal of building up the Lord's ekklesia, ministries will mostly end up building up their own groups.

The purpose of Galatians is to bring believers back to the practice of the Lord's ekklesia, where diverse believers can have meals and fellowship together in unity even though they keep their distinctions. That was the case in Antioch before Peter, and the rest of the Jews divided from these Gentile believers. They were having ekklesia together. The Lord's ekklesia in Antioch didn't belong to Paul, the Gentiles, Barnabas, Peter, or the Jews. **The ekklesia does not belong to any particular ministry**. Instead, she is a democratic assembly for all of God's people.

What happened in Antioch was described in detail in Romans 14. Paul described an assembly where both the Jewish and Gentile believers were in one place having a meal together. Many Jewish believers didn't eat certain foods, while Gentile believers ate everything. Therefore, there was a common propensity to judge one another. Paul's admonition was "do not pass judgment on one another" (Rom. 14:13), but welcome, receive and embrace one another just as Christ has received each of them, both Jews and Gentiles (Rom. 15:7).

Jewish believers should not try to convert the Gentiles to their Jewish convictions, nor should the Gentiles try to convert the Jewish believers to their opposing views. They are to accept each other no matter their convictions since each believer can have their perspectives before God: "Let us therefore make every effort to do what leads to peace and to mutual edification" (Rom. 14:5-8, 19, NIV). Ekklesia is the forum where each believer is welcomed without judgment, no matter their diversity. However, to not cause a problem with those with a contrary conviction, each should keep their conviction privately between themselves and God (Rom. 14:22).

The reality of the Lord's ekklesia is righteousness, peace, and joy in the Holy Spirit, which is the kingdom of God. The very essence of the kingdom is righteousness before God through faith, peace between diverse believers through the Lord's blood, and joy and rejoicing with God and men. They are to serve each other in such a way of being a peacemaker and that which builds up one another (Rom. 14:17-19). No matter the diversity of believers, no one should have an agenda to convert someone else to their perspective in the gathering of an ekklesia, but only to build up one another in peace for the kingdom of God. (Ministries often have a goal to help believers according to the assignments they believe they have received from God).

The description of the Lord's ekklesia is even more apparent in 1 Corinthians 11:17 through 14:40. Unlike a church or ministry, which cannot sustain opposing perspectives or divisions in its members, the ekklesia of the Lord needs believers from various factions to assemble and have meals together (1 Cor. 11:19). Secular democracies require participation from all sectors of society (rich, poor, business, soldiers, etc.) and would not function if only one particular class of people voted. Similarly, the Lord's ekklesia needs the participation of believers from opposing factions.

The only way to have unity with a divergent group of Christians is to remember the Lord together (1 Cor. 11:24-26). The Lord's supper was their center and focus: remembering the Lord. Elevating any other topic could cause debate and contention. However, there is one person in Whom all can agree Who is the reason for ekklesia: Jesus. Specifically, their common faith and salvation through Jesus Christ, the Son of God, Who died and resurrected as the Lord of all. When participating in the Lord's supper, each one is encouraged to discern that the Body of Christ is one: the "cup of thanksgiving" and the one bread is the one Body (1 Cor. 10:16-17).

Though diverse and different from one another, each member is appreciated, accepted, loved, and necessary (I Cor. 12 & 13). Finally, just as the bedrock of democracy is equal rights and freedom of speech, the Lord's ekklesia cannot be dominated, controlled, monopolized or manipulated by anyone or any ministry. Unlike churches, everyone has the right and privilege to speak their perspective and experiences of Christ one by one wherein no one can dominate the time (1 Cor. 14:26, 30-32).

This diversity in unity expresses the Trinity so that the unbelieving and uninformed in the ekklesia's gatherings can observe that God is present. After witnessing this unique unity, unbelievers will fall down and worship God with a believing heart (I Cor. 14:25). Such is a fulfillment of the Lord's prayer this divided world longs to see: "That they may all be one, just as you, Father, are in me, and I in you, that they also may be in us, so that the world may believe that you have sent me" (John 17:21).

7

THE NEW CREATION: THE ISRAEL OF GOD

The New Creation

> But far be it from me to boast except in the cross of our Lord Jesus Christ, by which the world has been crucified to me, and I to the world. For neither circumcision counts for anything, nor uncircumcision, but a **new creation**. And as for all who walk by this rule, peace and mercy be upon them, and upon the **Israel of God**.
>
> –Gal 6:14-16

Paul boasted or rejoiced in the cross of Christ because he was liberated from the "world." The world at the time of Paul was circumcision or uncircumcision. These two words, "circumcision and uncircumcision," represented two groups that immediately instigated cultural, political, and religious polarity. There was a vast divide between these two groups: the Jews who are circumcised and the Gentiles who are uncircumcised. Such was the wall of separation and hatred in the world of circumcision and uncircumcision.

The cross of Christ liberated Paul from the world of both circumcision or uncircumcision. He was not beholden or identified with either because the world was crucified to him — especially that "religious world." He could mingle and fellowship with people from both sides. The cross freed him from divisive religion, politics, and culture. He no longer belonged to the world of division, factions, hatred, intolerance, no-middle-ground, choose-your-side, and condemnation. Yes, the cross cleansed all our sins; however, no one can have absolute certainty experientially until judgment day. Nevertheless, the cross of Christ liberating believers from this divisive world that alienates people from one another can be observed and experienced today.

The practical working of the cross frees believers from the world of division and makes them alive to the New Creation — that's all that matters. Those living in the Spirit and who have Christ living in them are participants of His New Creation, which is the antithesis of the divisive world. The New Creation consists of people with contrary convictions: all of whom are one in Christ. They love one another and are yoked together to bear one another's burdens. Both circumcision and uncircumcision are not considered in the New Creation since both are nothing. Therefore, whether circumcised or uncircumcised, they value, accept, and love each other.

The "**rule** of the New Creation" means that the New Creation becomes the governing principle, and the regulating standard in the sphere of a believer's walk or living. Those walking by this rule of the New Creation bring peace into marriage, family, in-laws, fellow students, colleagues at work, and just about any environment. They are peacemakers. They are not affected by the divisive world around them because they live in the realm of the New Creation. This achievement of the cross of Christ is practical and effective here and now. Living the "crucified life" wherein "Christ lives in me" does not make a Christian "holier than thou." Instead, this person is humbled to bear the burdens of others, breaking down all divisive barriers.

Believers do not need to wait for the future to be in the New Creation. The New Creation is now: they can experience and enjoy the New Creation today. Jesus prayed in John 17 that His followers would not be taken out of this world (hostile and divisive as it is), but that they would be one, as one as the Father and the Son, so that the world would believe in the reality of Jesus Christ. The testimony of diversity in unity has to be on earth in the midst of a factious world. Such is the testimony of Jesus shining in this dark world.

Western value has preached diversity and acceptance in a democratic society. However, in the leading democratic nation, the USA, there is growing and persistent divisiveness, corruption, and hatred between those contrary to one another. Humanity cannot solve the problem of division since its root is sin. After Adam and Eve sinned by ingesting the forbidden fruit, the first act of sin was jealousy leading Cain to murder Abel: the ultimate of division. Since then, the bulk of world history has been more and more divisions and wars between people and nations. Divisiveness leading to war and murder is the ultimate expression of the old creation.

Jesus Christ's death and resurrection brought in the New Creation in the middle of this divisive world: the old creation.

> From now on, therefore, we regard no one according to the flesh. Even though we once regarded Christ according to the flesh, we regard him thus no longer. Therefore, if anyone is in Christ, he is a new creation. The old has passed away; behold, the new has come. All this is from God, who through Christ reconciled us to himself and gave us the ministry of reconciliation;
>
> —2 Cor. 5:16-18

The verse above is the only other Scripture that uses the phrase "New Creation." Faith is what brought believers into Jesus Christ. In Jesus Christ, old things are passed away, including the Old Man, fallen human nature, the flesh, and all its divisiveness, and they together constitute a New Creation.

It is enlightening to discover that with the New Creation is the ministry of reconciliation. Those in the New Creation have been reconciled to Christ. Now they have been given the ministry of reconciliation. They are the peacemakers bringing those divided into peace through the reconciliation made by Christ on the cross. The New Creation ministry is not merely about forgiving sins and going to heaven one day. Instead, it has everything to do with reconciling people to God and to one another.

Corinth is where Paul said they are fleshly babes because they are divided (1 Cor. 1:12-13; 3:1-4). In 2 Corinthians, the Judaizers attempted to separate the Corinthian believers from the apostle Paul who brought them to Christ. They sowed doubt regarding Paul's spiritual abilities by denigrating his appearance (flesh) (2 Cor. 5:12-16, 10:10). Therefore, Paul instructs them to "no longer regard anyone according to the flesh" as a means of avoiding division by the flesh (2 Cor. 5:16-21). The ministry of reconciliation guides people back to Christ — back to God — not being distracted by the differences in the flesh. Reconciliation between divided people is impossible outside of God through Christ. Therefore, whoever is brought back to Christ is positioned to be at peace with all people.

In Galatians, Paul was doing his best, struggling and laboring to bring both the circumcised and the uncircumcised back to Jesus Christ and His Cross. It is by the works of the flesh that these Galatian believers were divided; however, it is in the New Creation that they are united.

March in Rank by the Rule of the New Creation

> For neither circumcision counts for anything, nor uncircumcision, but a new creation. And as for all who walk by this rule, peace and mercy be upon them, and upon the Israel of God.
>
> –Gal 6:15-16

The New Creation should be a rule or standard by which all should walk. Rather than walking by the laws of Moses, rules of holiness, regulations, or limitations of any Christian brand, believers need to walk by the rule of the New Creation as explained above: oneness in Christ with all diverse believers.

The word for "walk" in Greek is "*stoicheō*," which has the meaning of "march in military rank" (Strong's), or "to proceed in a row, go in order" (Thayer's). It is a military word describing a fighting unit moving together in one accord like a phalanx, lined up tightly in a row (BDAG). In God's kingdom, all believers are in one fighting force. No matter the backgrounds, preferences, or even convictions — once people are part of an army, they march (fight and move) as one. They join together to fight a common enemy. An army consists of many individual soldiers, but they must fight as one man.

Whether circumcised or uncircumcised, Catholic or Protestant, Baptist or Pentecostal, Reformed or charismatic, Republican or Democrat, rich or poor, black or white, Chinese or American, male or female: each Christian needs to be governed by the New Creation, march in the same steps in one accord, which is the only way to fight and defeat Satan, the enemy, the great divider (Matt. 16:18; Phil. 1:27-28). Peace and mercy upon all those marching by the rule of the New Creation. Peace between those previously divided and mercy is better than sacrifice.

> If we live by the Spirit, let us also **keep in step** with the Spirit. Let us not become conceited, provoking one another, envying one another.
>
> –Gal. 5:25-26

In Galatians 5:25, Paul used the same word, "*stoicheō*," meaning "keep in step" with the Spirit. All those who have life or live by the Spirit should march in step with the Spirit. The Spirit's goal is the New Creation. Therefore, marching in step with the Spirit is marching according to the rule of the New Creation. The Spirit's goal is not merely for the individual believer's victory and holiness. Instead, the Spirit has the same goal as the Lord Jesus when He said He would build His ekklesia: that His people will be one. Since the Lord Jesus and the Spirit are one, their goal is identical: His diverse people becoming one in the Trinity. Again, not "organizationally one" (i.e., ecumenism) but oneness via the very fellowship of the Triune God into Whom we have entered in fellowship, life, and glory.

Peace and Mercy

> . . . as for all who walk by this rule, peace and mercy be upon them, and upon the Israel of God.
>
> –Gal. 6:16, ESV
>
> Peace and mercy will come to rest on all those who conform to this principle. They are the Israel of God.
>
> –Gal. 6:16, GW

Peace be upon those walking by the rule of the New Creation. Peace as defined in the New Testament is not merely the absence of conflict, peace by definition includes: harmony, security, prosperity, tranquility, and happiness. What a blessing it is to be in peace!

Jesus broke down the middle wall of hostility between the Jews and the Gentiles to create in Himself one New Man; thus, making peace. Then Paul continued: Jesus came back in His resurrection to preach peace (Eph. 2:17). He preached to those far-off (Gentiles) and those near (Jews) so that they might become one in the Father through Him. Today, believers should be wary of divisive preaching. Instead, they should participate in the gospel of peace: preaching peace to those divided from each other. Thus, bringing them back to the Father for the sake of the New Creation: the New Man. This peace of which we speak entails not only one's personal peace through salvation, but also "reconciling peace" through the same "blood of the cross" with your brothers and sisters.

It is under the feet of those in peace that God crushes Satan. "The God of peace shall soon crush Satan under your feet" (Rom. 16:20). In Romans 16, believers in Rome were greeting each other with no concern for which group they may have identified. They proactively went to each other to initiate fellowship. Instead of staying separated in their groups, they began and continued having fellowship with each other, thus breaking down the boundaries of group identity. This peace is upon all those marching by the rule of the New Creation.

> For judgment is without mercy to one who has shown no mercy. Mercy triumphs over judgment.
>
> —James 2:13
>
> Go and learn what this means: 'I desire mercy, and not sacrifice.' For I came not to call the righteous, but sinners.
>
> —Matt. 9:13

Mercy is upon those marching by the rule of the New Creation. The meaning of "mercy" according to *Vine's* is "the outward manifestation of pity; it assumes need on the part of him who receives it, and resources adequate to meet the need on the part of him who shows it." All believers in their Christian journey would certainly welcome God's mercy. Is anyone so proud that they want God to judge them strictly based on their works? Instead, everyone with a sober mind should want God to show mercy. How happy is our heart every time we sing the old hymn "Great is Thy faithfulness . . . morning by morning new mercies I see!" Mercy is what believers receive when coming boldly to the throne of grace (Heb. 4:16).

This mercy references Romans 11 wherein Paul speaks of the "one olive tree" with two branches — of Jews and Gentiles becoming one in Christ. "For God has committed them all [both Jew and Gentile] in disobedience, that He might have mercy on all" (Rom. 11:32, NKJV). God's mercy is given to all so that we would present our very bodies for His one Body (Rom. 12:3-6).

As believers march (move and fight) in step by the rule or principle of the New Creation, they will find themselves bonding with others who have different perspectives and experiences. In judgmental environments, it is impossible to keep a tight rank as a phalanx with a diverse group of believers. When a person says or does something irksome or offensive, they either judge and therefore separate from the offending one or show mercy.

Much mercy must be shown, in doing so, God's mercy abides upon all those showing mercy to their fellow believers.

When the Pharisees condemned Jesus for eating with sinners and tax collectors, Jesus said that He was there as a physician among sinners. He was showing mercy by being with them. He then quoted from the Hebrew Scriptures that God desires mercy and not sacrifice (Hosea 6:6; Matt. 9:13). Religious people often display their piety and holiness as a sacrifice to God. However, God doesn't want their sacrifices from their direct devotions to Him. He would prefer they show mercy to those they considered to be sinners. When the Pharisees separated themselves from sinners, they considered this a sacrifice to God. Similarly, due to their devotion to God, many believers separate themselves from "sinners" as a display of sacrificing to God. However, Jesus mingled with the sinners to show mercy.

Back in Galatians 2, all these Gentile believers were labeled "sinners." So, if they were to march by the rule of the New Creation, these Jewish believers would have shown mercy and eaten together with these sinners. This demonstration of mercy upon the Gentiles — and upon all those contrary to each other — will cause God's mercy to be with those who march by the New Creation.

The Israel of God

At the close of his epistle to the Galatians, Paul used the phrase "Israel of God." Israel means "he will rule as God" (Strong's). He described the New Creation in Galatians 6:15 as the "Israel of God" in Galatians 6:16. The Israel of God has nothing to do with circumcision or uncircumcision. Rather, she is the New Creation God desired from Abraham's time. In other words, if all that "avails" is the New Creation, then "peace and mercy" can only be upon those walking in this manner: they are "the Israel of God."[9] It is significant for Paul to conclude with the phrase Israel of God since these Jewish believers undoubtedly exclusively considered themselves the true Israel of God with genuine lineage from Abraham. They perceived themselves as guardians of God's law, manifesting God's rule on the earth. With this understanding and zeal, they were motivated to convert Gentiles

---

9   Some use Galatians 6:16 to support their view that only believing Jews should retain the title of the "Israel of God." Those who hold this view find validation in the Amplified Version translation of Galatians 6:16: "Peace and mercy be upon all who walk by this rule, and upon the [true] Israel of God [Jewish believers]" (Gal. 6:16, AMP).

to be part of the blessed "Israel." The conviction that they were the rightful representative of Israel, the beloved and chosen people, was the reason they separated from Gentile believers — who in their eyes had nothing to do with "the Israel of God" because, for one, they were not circumcised.

These Jewish Christians had the following attitude toward Gentile Christians:

It is good that you have Jesus as Lord with His redemption. We have the same Jesus you have, but we have something more: we are the direct descendants of Israel, the people to rule on behalf of God on earth. Therefore, convert and be part of Israel. Inwardly, Judaizers felt that at best what these believers in Jesus possessed was but a half salvation if at all! As a Gentile, it would have been tempting to convert by becoming "circumcised." Why remain as a mere believer in Jesus when one can also rule as God's exclusive representative?

Paul used this entire epistle to clarify and conclude what the Israel of God is in the New Testament: **The New Creation is now the Israel of God** — comprised of both Jew and those called out from among the nations; the Gentiles. These two verses were a punctuation mark at the close of his letter.

While the Judaizers were "forcing" the Gentiles to convert to be part of the Israel of the flesh (Gal. 2:14), in actuality, the Judaizers were Ishmael of Hagar, Abraham's illegitimate son under slavery. Additionally, they were the persecutors of those enjoying grace, those liberated in Christ. Since the Judaizers representing the Jewish Christian sect is not "all Israel" (Rom. 11:26) did the Israel of God cease to exist? The Jewish believers may ask: if not us, then who?

Throughout history, Christian groups have considered themselves "chosen" or "special" in some way. This special designation could be due to various blessings God bestowed. These groups may possess some especially helpful doctrines, a key for unlocking spiritual gifts, unique methods of holiness, zeal to bring people to Christ, or even a passion for cultivating the presence of God. Like Judaizers, each of these groups can claim God's favor upon them and compel other Christians to join them and receive the same blessings.

Such zeal to share these blessings comes from a caring and loving heart for their fellow believers. However, their sharing can morph into a kind of preaching aimed at converting other Christians to join their group. This preaching can start innocently but soon create separation and division from those they deem inferior. These groups will consider other Christians enemies who do not understand their perspective or challenge their agenda of spreading their doctrine or practice.

Therefore, understanding Galatians gives believers tools to stop this repeating cycle in history. Indeed, all Christians should continually seek God and search the Scriptures as they move forward in their journey for God's purpose. Nevertheless, when God answers and the Spirit moves, don't fall for the temptation to build another enlightened group. Don't persecute God's people by alienating other believers who have not received similar blessings. Galatians helps Christians from becoming the "Judaizers" of today, thinking only their group is building up God's kingdom and that unless and until believers adhere to your particular "Christian brand" they will somehow "miss out" on "kingdom blessings."

In Romans 14, Paul says diverse believers, including those weak in the faith, are necessary for building up God's kingdom. The approved and acceptable ministers serve righteousness, peace, and joy of the Holy Spirit to all believers without bias. They make peace between believers who hold contrary convictions. Instead of trying to build up a special group of believers who are "like-minded," these peacemakers model a pattern for fellowshipping with all kinds of believers, no matter how diverse they may be. They facilitate the manifestation of the Lord's ekklesia — the New Creation — which is the Israel of God.

Conclusion of Galatians

The gospel of Jesus Christ is the foundational bulwark of Christianity. What do Christians actually preach as the good news of God? What do people really believe in order to receive salvation? What is the result when a person comes to faith and becomes a Christian, a follower of Jesus Christ? These are fundamental questions every believer should clearly understand.

There is little controversy among Christians that this is the gospel: Jesus Christ is God come in the flesh (the Son of God became man). He was a perfect, sinless man Who died to redeem sinful man. He resurrected on the third day and ascended as the Lord of all. Every person believing and calling out to Jesus as Lord and Savior is justified (righteous) before God, receives eternal life, and the indwelling Spirit who is also Jesus Christ lives in such a person. No matter how much people differ in race, gender, socio-economic status, culture, or politics, they share this gospel as their common faith (Titus 1:4), granting each a common salvation (Jude 1:3), whereby they enjoy their commonwealth (Eph. 2:12-13).

Most bible teachers and students have missed Jesus Christ's ultimate goal of the gospel. His goal is to bring once divided people into one New Man — His one Body — which is His Ekklesia. Unity has not been an emphasis of the gospel among Christians. Most Christians think only of their personal salvation: "I am saved, are you?" Therefore, most are ignorant to the truth that division from other believers is against the gospel of Jesus Christ. Conflicting views among God's people are inevitable. For believers to walk in the truth of the gospel, they must stay in fellowship with one another, even with those holding diverse and contrary perspectives and experiences. This gospel of peace needs to be preached to divided believers.

Galatians exposes how the gospel has been distorted or perverted, and this distortion is designed to divide God's people. Satan has even used God's law and blessings upon His people to cause division, separation, and alienation. This subtlety of Satan's craftiness that uses men of God to cause divisions must be exposed to all Christians.

The Judaizers were narrow-minded, thinking their Jewish faction of believers was the only ones chosen as the Israel of God to carry on God's testimony. Similarly, Christians have done the same over the centuries. Consider how many men God has used to help His people in spiritual renewal. Even so, purposely or not, their followers have borne their brand (viz. the mark of circumcision). These various brands have divided and segregated God's people. Though used by God, those in their respective marks of circumcision have been zealous to convert other Christians into their doctrinal perspectives or Christian practices.

This zeal to convert other Christians to bear their mark has resulted in preaching a distorted or perverted gospel. They have preached Jesus Christ plus something else. Faith in Jesus Christ alone has not been sufficient. They insist that Christians also must follow certain laws to become more devoted and holy. This distortion even affected the apostle Peter where he took the lead to separate and divide from these Gentile believers in Antioch: he didn't walk according to the truth of the gospel.

Christ died so that all God's people are liberated into grace. No matter which brand or none at all, all believers are justified in the same way by faith. They are all crucified with Christ and with Christ living in them. Therefore, they should not be distracted by any law or tempted to use their self-energy (flesh) to fulfill God's requirements.

Each believer should continue in the supply of the Spirit and bear the fruit of the Spirit that they may receive, love, and bear the burdens of other believers, especially those who are contrary and different — even "someone caught in a sin" should be restored with gentleness and humility (Gal. 6:1). The only rule or measurement to which each believer should march in step is with the New Creation. God will pour out His blessings of peace and mercy upon them as we march in unity with our diverse brothers and sisters in Christ.

Contrary to most Christians' understanding, Galatians primarily focuses on advancing the truth of the gospel to build up the Lord's ekklesia — His Body — which Paul (as Saul) tried to destroy. The result of any distortion or perversion of the gospel is division. Galatians outlines Paul's struggle to "preach Christ and Him crucified." The death and resurrection of Jesus Christ accomplished everything needed to give all spiritual blessings to God's people[10]. Here are a few of the blessings listed in Galatians for the building up of His one Body:

- Justification by faith (Gal. 2:16)
- The old "I" crucified: This is the self-identity of the old creation (Gal. 2:20)
- Christ living and indwelling His believers (Gal. 2:20)
- His believers walking and living in the good land of the Spirit (Gal. 3:14, 5:25)
- Christ broke down every dividing wall of hostility between peoples and made them one (Gal. 3:28)
- His diverse people marching (moving and fighting) together by the rule of the New Creation (Gal. 6:15-16)
- He supplied the fruit of the Spirit (Gal. 5:22-23)
- Building up the eternal Israel of God: His ekklesia (Gal. 6:16)

Therefore, let us not exult in the "mark of the flesh" — either in circumcision or uncircumcision — but as Paul: ". . . for I bear on my body the marks of Jesus." We should bear the same marks He bore for us on that cross. The "mark of circumcision," or for that matter, no mark at all, means

---

10 His people include circumcision, uncircumcision, slaves, masters, male, female, Jews, and Gentiles.

absolutely nothing; it counts for nothing. Bearing the "marks of Jesus" is to live in the reality of all that Jesus Christ accomplished on the cross, marching (moving and fighting) in step by the New Creation, God's Ekklesia (Gal. 6:17).

> "The grace of our Lord Jesus Christ be with your spirit, brothers and sisters. Amen"
>
> (Gal. 6:18).

BONUS:
CONCERNING ALL ISRAEL

The Restoration of Israel: The United Kingdom of David

The letter to the Galatians was written within a few years[11] (maybe three years) after the Jerusalem Council in Acts 15, which settled the issue that Gentile believers do not need to be circumcised and come under the law of Moses. Paul recited this event at the beginning of Galatians 2. That Council had a momentous conclusion by James. Paul's closing with the Israel of God was synchronized and supported by James in Acts 15. In fact, Galatians could be Paul's exposition of James' conclusion regarding the rebuilding of the Tabernacle or United Kingdom of David.

What James summarized concluding the Council regarding the "yoke of circumcision" being placed upon the Goyim (Gentiles) who believed "into" Jesus Christ was the fulfillment of the prophecy found in Amos 9:10-11 (quoted by James). The realization of this prophecy was not expected in the distant future but the "here and now." The inclusion of the nations (the Goyim), into the Lord's Ekklesia was also the fulfillment that "Jesus would die for the Jewish nation, and not only for that nation but also for the scattered children of God, to bring them together and make them one" (John 11:52 NIV).

The Council in Jerusalem was initiated by the ekklesia ("church") in Antioch. Antioch was the first ekklesia of the Lord recorded among the Gentiles and the launching point for Paul's missionary journeys to the Gentiles. Therefore, Antioch likely represented the concerns of all Gentile believers. Jewish believers (Judaizers) were traveling to wherever Paul had

---

11 There is controversy concerning the date when this epistle was written and whether it was to the north or south Galatia. This book has taken the traditional view: The date is around AD 53-54, after the council in Jerusalem in Acts 15. Nevertheless, whether it was before the Jerusalem council or after (around AD 50), it does not matter as far as the basic thesis of this book, which is that Galatians was written to solve the problem of division among believers. However, if it was written before the Jerusalem council then this author would apologize to apostle Peter for being too harsh on him. A good discussion for dating this epistle: The Date and Destination of Galatians | Bible.org

established ekklesia. These Jewish followers of Jesus were telling Gentile believers that unless they were circumcised, they could not be saved (Acts 15:1, 24). This confab in Jerusalem included all the apostles, elders, and the whole ekklesia, including a contingent of Pharisees who believed in Christ. The Jewish believers, with their center in Jerusalem, were fervent for the law. Although they eventually agreed that Gentile believers did not need to be under the law of Moses, they stayed on the same trajectory until seemingly the majority of Christians in Jerusalem were zealous for the law (Acts 21:20).

After much dispute, questioning and reasoning, concerning the matter of the Gentiles coming under the law, Peter testified what he witnessed at the household of Cornelius, the Gentile Roman (no less) centurion: they were filled with the Spirit the same as the Jews experienced on Pentecost. Since they were saved the same way, these Jewish believers should not put a yoke of the law on them that even the Jews themselves couldn't bear and fulfill (". . . a yoke that neither we nor our ancestors have been able to bear?" Acts 15:10). Barnabas and Paul also gave their testimony concerning how God moved among the Gentiles with miracles and wonders as He did in Jerusalem.

Finally, James decisively concluded without rebuttals from anyone. His conclusion was astonishing and momentous. He applied this amazing prophecy in the Hebrew Scriptures from Amos 9:11-12 to this dilemma which could have only been a direct enlightenment and revelation by the Holy Spirit.

> The words of the prophets agree completely with this. As the scripture says, 'After this I will return, says the Lord, and restore the kingdom (tabernacle) of David. I will rebuild its ruins and make it strong again. And so all the rest of the human race will come to me, all the Gentiles whom I have called to be my own. So says the Lord, who made this known long ago.'
> —Acts 15:16-17 GNT

James concluded that the Gentiles and Jews coming together in Christ fulfills the prophecy for the restoration of the Kingdom of David. It is necessary to go back in history to understand this shocking statement and learn when the kingdom of David disintegrated into "ruins." Understanding how, when, and why the ten northern tribes (also called Israel, Ephraim, Jezreel, Samaria) divided from the two southern tribes (Benjamin and Judah – collectively called Judah and eventually the Jews) and whatever happened to these ten northern tribes, will expand our understanding of God's eternal plan and purpose of the ages.

Saul was the first king of Israel. God chose Saul and then rejected him due to his multiple failures and replaced him with King David, a man after God's own heart. King David united all of Israel under one kingdom (tabernacle) and defeated all the enemies in the promised land. Additionally, after seven years of His united reign over all Israel, he made Jerusalem the capital and prepared everything for the building up of God's temple during his 33-year reign from Jerusalem (2 Sam. 5:5). His heart was to have a dwelling place of God (1 Sam. 7:2-4). He was a type of the coming Jesus Christ – the Son of David (Matt. 1:1). Therefore, the prophecy concerning Jesus Christ used the name of David (Jer. 30:9; Ezek. 34:23). The Kingdom of David is a foretelling of the Kingdom of Jesus Christ – "Jesus the Messiah the son of David."

David desired to build a house for God's dwelling, and so he bought a site, designed it, and prepared all the material in a place eventually named "the City of David," but God said he could not build it. The actual building was left to Solomon, his son. Solomon finished building the Temple (God's house). The United Kingdom of David (Israel) was at its zenith – all twelve tribes were under "David's Tent" or "Tabernacle." God came and filled the Solomonic Temple with His glory; the nations of the earth brought tribute and heard the wisdom of Solomon (1 Kings 4:21, 34).

However, Solomon married many "foreign wives" – they turned his heart away from God to their idols (1 Kings 11:3-4). Therefore, God judged Solomon and broke up the United Kingdom David had established into two parts: the ten tribes of the north called Israel (aka Ephraim, Jezreel, Samaria), and Judah with Benjamin made up the Southern Kingdom (1 Kings 11:26-43). This split took place during the reign of Solomon's son Rehoboam. With the ten northern tribes, Jeroboam came to King Rehoboam to request a reduction in taxes and stop exploiting their free labor. Rehoboam rejected their request; instead of reducing taxes, he said he would increase them. This event caused an irreparable split ending the reign of the United Kingdom of David. Then the ten northern tribes separated, and the United Kingdom of David fell into ruins until the coming of Jesus Christ, almost 1000 years later.

Although it was God's plan to split up the United Kingdom of David into ten and two tribes. He still desired all twelve tribes to continue feasting and worshipping before Him as one man in Jerusalem. They could be under two kings with different administrations, but they still needed to enjoy feasting together before Him as one people. There remains one temple, one priesthood, one law, and all twelve tribes gathered to celebrate in oneness before God three times a year.

It was God's plan to make Jeroboam king over the ten tribes; nevertheless, Jeroboam was ambitious and didn't trust God's plan. He reasoned that if the ten tribes went up to Jerusalem in Judah's territory to worship, their hearts would turn back to Judah. Thus, he would lose his kingship over the ten tribes (1 Kings 12:27). Therefore, he devised a plan to set up two idols in two worship centers with his priests (one in upper Israel – Dan; and the other in Ephraim bordering next to the Tribe of Benjamin). King Jeroboam told Israel they did not need to travel the long journey to Jerusalem to offer sacrifices to God. They could now worship in their own territory. This systemic and institutionalized division of God's people using idolatry was a significant offense to God. Therefore, the phrase "God remembered the sins of Jeroboam" appears repeatedly in the Hebrew Scriptures.

The ten northern tribes had several names throughout Hebrew Scripture: Israel and Ephraim were the two prominent ones. The southern two tribes were called Judah. Israel, the northern kingdom, spiraled into worsening degradation until God used Assyria to judge them. The systemic division in the kingdom of David eventually resulted in the Ten Tribes (Israel, Ephraim) being deported to Assyria and the two tribes of Judah and Benjamin taken into Babylonian captivity (aka, the Seventy Years of Babylonian Captivity – BC 608-537). The Assyrian Empire occupied about 120 nations at the time of Ephraim's full deportation (cir. BC 745-712). The ten tribes of Israel were scattered throughout the Assyrian Empire and were assimilated[12] – "*Israel is swallowed up; now they are among the Nations*" (Hosea 8:7-8). That is the reason *Ephraim* became synonymous with the *Nations* (Gen. 48:19; Hosea 1:10; 2:23; 8:7-8; Acts 15:14, 17).

When the Assyrians defeated and conquered a tribe or nation, their strategy was to swap out the population, scatter the conquered people, and assimilate them among the Assyrian's vast empire. Assyria did so

---

12 https://www.britannica.com/topic/Jew-people

to Israel — she was swallowed up among the nations and "Now they are among the Nations/Gentiles" (Hos. 8:8-9). After both Israel and ultimately Judah were defeated, Israel's population was deported to the Assyrian Empire, and Judah was eventually deported to Babylon. By human and historical terms, the once flourishing United Kingdom of David should have been gone forever. The ten tribes were essentially gone, swallowed up, just as the great fish "swallowed up" Jonah (same Hebrew word: *bala*). They didn't just get lost to be found one day. They literally disappeared and were assimilated into the nations. Search as you may, their DNA is simply diffused among the nations.[13]

By the time of their deportation, Israel (the ten tribes) had already stopped worshipping Yahweh in Jerusalem, given up the Levites as their priests, and ignored the law of Moses for nearly 300 years (all 19 of their kings were considered "evil" in the eyes of the Lord). Therefore, they were ready to be assimilated by the nations. Nevertheless, Judah stayed distinct and separate from the nations due to the Temple and the Levites' guidance in keeping the law.

Therefore, even after being carried off to Babylon, faithful believers like Daniel and his companions kept the Jews intact as a people in a foreign land. God kept His promise that Judah would someday return to the promised land after 70 years in captivity (BC 608-537; Jer. 25:11-12; 29:10). Therefore, a small remnant of about 50,000 people of Judah and Benjamin and a contingent of Levites went back to Jerusalem — with scarcely a few Israelites. These Jews who went back considered themselves to represent Israel (Neh. 7:73). The Jews who returned from Babylon became Israel, and the other ten tribes were no more. The United Kingdom of David, with her twelve tribes, had disintegrated — the Tabernacle of David was in ruins!

According to Jeremiah 3:8: "I gave faithless Israel her certificate of divorce and sent her away because of all her adulteries. Yet I saw that her unfaithful sister Judah had no fear; she also went out and committed adultery." "Faithless Israel" was given a "certificate of divorce" by Yahweh, but Judah was not. No doubt the prophecy given by Jacob (Israel) in Genesis

---

13 Virtually all modern-day Israeli scholarship concludes that the ten northern tribes were assimilated among the nations and are considered "lost" for all intents and purposes. Even so, some 200+ years elapsed between the Assyrian deportation of the ten northern tribes (BC 744-711) to the initial Babylonian captivities (BC 608-586) with the return of approximately 50,000 Jews from Babylonian Captivity to Judah (cir., BC 537-38).

49:10 persists in that: "The scepter will not depart from Judah, nor the ruler's staff from between his feet, until he to whom it belongs shall come (i.e. 'until Shiloh comes')."

Gentiles Represent the Ten "Lost" Tribes

Back to Acts 15, the purpose of the conference was related to whether Gentile believers needed to become Jewish by circumcision. Seemingly out of nowhere, James quoted a prophecy from Amos and declared that the Gentiles and the Jews coming together in Christ is the fulfillment of biblical prophecy — it was the rebuilding of the United Kingdom of David with all twelve tribes under King David's Tabernacle, booth or tent

Absolutely mind blowing: yes, these Gentile believers are the dispersed and swallowed-up ten northern tribes.

James made the critical conclusion at this monumental assembly by quoting the prophecy from the Hebrew Scriptures (Amos 9:11-12). What was taking place between the Jewish believers and "those scattered among the nations" (aka, the Gentiles) was the prophetic fulfillment of the restoration of the United Kingdom of David and the "uniting bond of peace" through the blood of Christ.

According to James, these Gentiles are really "scattered Israel." Now, through faith in Christ, the United Kingdom of David is being rebuilt: "Its ruins I will rebuild, and I will restore it" (Acts 15:16). Some well-meaning brethren believe that David's Tabernacle — His United Kingdom — will not manifest until the Millennial Reign of the Son of David. That's not what James was saying or what the Jerusalem Council so strongly affirmed. It was happening NOW.

This understanding parallels John's prophetic word in John 11:51-52 when he said, ". . . Jesus would die for the [Jewish] nation . . . but also that He would gather together in one the children of God who were scattered abroad." The children scattered are the Gentiles. Christ's death on the cross was to bring those scattered (Gentiles) together with the Jewish believers and make them one. The phrase "the children of God" used in John 11:51-52 is also found in John 1:12: "But as many as received Him to them gave

He the authority (the power or right) to become the children of God, even to them who believe on His name." Thus, the "children of God" (Gk. *teknon*) are all those believing "into" His name — whosoever will — meaning, all the "children of God scattered" throughout the nations.

The Judaizers considered themselves the only Israel of God and chosen heir upholding God's glory. That was the reason they were zealous in their attempt to convert the Gentile believers. Instead, Paul exposed them to be Ishmael, a slave and not the heir. The real Israel of God is the New Creation in Christ — that's all that avails anything — consisting of all diverse people, including both Jews and Gentiles. The Israel of God in Galatians fulfills the promise to Abraham, the father of faith, that "in His seed shall all the nations be blessed" (Gen. 18:18). It is also the fulfillment of Jacob's blessing upon Ephraim (the son of Joseph from his Egyptian wife): his offspring shall become a "multitude of nations" (Gen. 48:19).

Consider these promises made by God to Abraham, Isaac, Jacob, and Ephraim which has to do with the inclusion of the nations:

> God's promise to Abraham: "Behold, my covenant is with you, and you shall be the father of a multitude of nations"
>
> –Gen. 17:4
>
> (Note: "multitude of nations" literally means: "Fullness of the Gentiles" or "Nations")
>
> God's promise to Isaac: "I will make your offspring as numerous as the stars of the sky, I will give your offspring all these lands, and all the nations of the earth will be blessed by your offspring,"
>
> –Gen. 26:4, CSB
>
> God's promise to Israel (Jacob) when He changed his name: "And God said to him, 'I am God Almighty; be fruitful and increase in number. A nation and a community of nations [literally "fullness of the nations"] will come from you, and kings will be among your descendants."
>
> –Gen. 35:11

Jacob/Israel purposely switched and crossed hands putting his right hand upon Ephraim as he prophesied:

> "He [Manasseh] too will become great. Nevertheless, his younger brother [Ephraim] will be greater than he, and his descendants will become a group of nations (NIV but most translations render this as "a multitude of nations") . . . So he put Ephraim ahead of Manasseh."
>
> –Gen. 48:19-20

Esau, Whom God Hated, Is Included

This coming together in oneness will cause the rest of mankind (human race) to come to the Lord. This is the fulfillment of the Lord's prayer in John 17: The world will believe when the followers of Jesus are one (John 17:21). The word "mankind" was used in Acts 15:17 but in Amos 9:11-12 the word "mankind" is not used but the word "Edom" is used. "Edom is Esau" (Gen. 36:1) — the estranged brother of Jacob, whom God hated (Rom. 9:13). Yet, just a few verses later, the merciful God said: "Those who were not my people I will call 'my people,' and her who was not beloved I will call 'beloved'" (Rom. 9:25). God could not be boxed-in.

> And the ark of God remained with the household of Obed-Edom in his house three months. And the LORD blessed the household of Obed-Edom and all that he had.
>
> –1 Chron. 13:14

> And also Obed-Edom and his sixty-eight brothers, while Obed-Edom, the son of Jeduthun, and Hosah were to be gatekeepers.
>
> –1 Chron. 16:38

Before the Ark of the Covenant was placed in the tabernacle of David in Jerusalem, that Ark did abide in the Household of Obed-Edom for three months, and God greatly blessed his household.

Obed-Edom means "Servant of Edom." He was clearly an Edomite. Although 1 Chronicles records that God hated Esau/Edom, we learn that Obed-Edom, along with 68 of his Edomite relatives, and his Edomite associate, Hosah, followed the Ark of the Covenant into the Tabernacle of David and became Levitical priests, serving as "gatekeepers." He was one of the sons of Jeduthun, who were chosen and designated by name to give thanks to the LORD. The sons of Jeduthun were stationed at the gate. They were responsible for sounding of the trumpets and cymbals and playing the other instruments for sacred songs. (1 Chron. 16:39-42 NIV).

That is how all-inclusive the Tabernacle of David was, and the Kingdom of Christ is today. Do you see the United Kingdom of David?

This story of Obed-Edom foreshadows James' declaration that when the Tabernacle of David is rebuilt, which is the joining together of Gentiles and Jews in Christ, then the rest of humankind will come to the Lord (Acts 15:15-16). This is the critical magnitude of the oneness of the Body of Christ!

BIBLIOGRAPHY

Anders, Max. *Holman New Testament Commentary - Galatians, Ephesians, Philippians, Colossians (Volume 8)*. Holman Reference

Arichea, Daniel C. , Eugene A. Nida. *A Handbook on Paul's Letter to the Galatians*. United Bible Society

Arndt, W., Danker, F. W., Bauer, W., & Gingrich, F. W. (2000). In *A Greek-English lexicon of the New Testament and other early Christian literature* (3rd ed., p. 946). University of Chicago Press.

Bruce, F. F. *The Epistle to the Galatians (The New International Greek Testament Commentary)*. NY, NY: Eerdmans New York

Coneybeare and Howson. *The Life and Epistles of St. Paul*. Grand Rapid, MI: WM. B. Eerdmans Publishing Co.

Dockery, David S. *Holman Concise Bible Commentary*. Holman Reference

George, Timothy. *Galatians: An Exegetical and Theological Exposition of Holy Scripture (Volume 30) (The New American Commentary)*. Holman Reference

Jamieson, Robert, A.R. Fausset, et al.. *Commentary Critical and Explanatory on the Whole Bible*. R&R Computer Solutions

Krieger, Douglas W., *So You Want to do Ekklesia?*. Sacramento, CA: Tribnet Publications, 2020

Krieger, Douglas W., *The United Kingdom of David...That they all may be One*. Sacramento, CA: Tribnet Publications, 2021

Lee, Witness. *Life-Study on Galatians*. Anaheim, CA: Living Stream Ministry

Lange, Johann Peter, et al. *A Commentary on the Holy Scriptures: Galatians*. Faithlife

Lenski, Richard C. H. *Interpretation of St Paul's Epistle to Galatians (Lenski's Commentary on the New Testament)*. Minneapolis, MN: Fortress Press

Richards, Lawrence O. *The Teacher's Commentary*. Victor Books

Stott, John. *The Message of Galatians (The Bible Speaks Today Series)*. London, UK: IVP Academic

Thayer, Joseph Henry. *Thayer's Greek–English Lexicon of the New Testament*. NY, NY: Harper & Brothers

Vine's W. E. *Vine's Expository Dictionary of New Testament Words*. Nashville, TN: Thomas Nelson

Walvoord, John F. and Roy B. Zuck. *Bible Knowledge Commentary (2 Volume Set) (Bible Knowledge Series)*. Colorado Springs, CO: David C. Cook

BOOKS BY HENRY HON

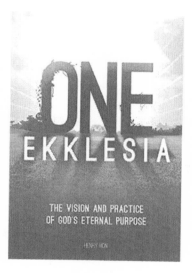

The Vision and Practice of God's Eternal Purpose: ONE EKKLESIA is not about how to improve your church, leave your church, or to start a better church. Rather, its vision and practice are to fulfill the Lord's prayer for His people (whether attending church or not) to be ONE so the world will believe. It is a practical oneness of diverse believers impacting the world. This will ignite the holy fire of God spreading uncontrollably . . . the next and final revival.

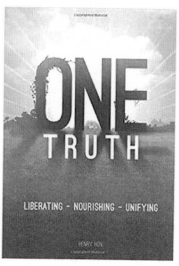

Liberating – Nourishing – Unifying: Jesus said: The truth shall set you free and if the Son sets you free, you shall be free for real. When Jesus declared these words in John 8, the religious people of His day were first condemning an adulterous woman to death, then after Jesus saved her, they wanted to kill Jesus.

Truth liberates people from religious condemnation and its zeal that's ready to kill — if not physically then at least psychologically or spiritually.

The word "truth" in the Greek (*alethia*) means "the reality lying at the basis of appearance." People are caught up with appearances both in the secular and religious world. There is a hunger within every person for what is real. Your inner being is drained by vanity; truth is needed to nourish, sustain and energize your soul. The world is full of hostile separations. Jesus in John 17 gave the gift of truth so that the most hostile and divided people may become united. Religious dogma and ceremonial practices divide, but truth unites.

A person who has received logic and life from truth is one who can love, forgive, and express kindness to all; especially, those different or contrary to himself. Jesus answered: "I am the way, the TRUTH, and the life" (John 14:6).

Bonus: Introducing the *Completion Gospel*, which is needed today for the ending of the age. Most of the gospel heard by people today is basically only half of it. The entire gospel needs to be preached! **ONE TRUTH**. Now in AUDIO @ www.onebody.life.

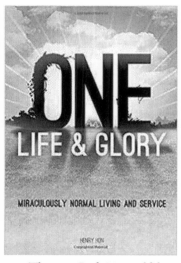

Miraculously Normal Living and Service . . . Both Christians and non-Christians like to witness the supernatural, miraculous actions taken by God. Certainly, God can do miracles to heal your loved ones from terminal diseases or to solve all your financial worries with a lottery winning. However, God's desire with humanity is not to be their "Santa Claus"; His desire and purpose is wonderful beyond imagination: He wants to be "miraculously normal" in humanity. Not just hit and miss miraculous events here and there, but miraculous every day, such that it is normal and ordinary.

This is God Himself being the source, empowering humanity to live by His divine-eternal life through faith in Jesus Christ. Being miraculously normal means: it will be indistinguishable whether it is you or God who is loving, caring, forgiving, enduring, and living in this present world. Moreover, services rendered to both God and humanity can likewise be miraculously normal.

Ordinary words can be spoken; yet, they can give eternal life to the hearer. Through normal interactions, peace can be made between people previously divided and hostile with one another; they are brought into fellowship. This book, *One in Life and Glory*, is the third in this series forming a Trilogy together with: *One Ekklesia* and *One Truth*. This Trilogy of *ONE* expounds on the Lord's prayer in John 17 for all His people to become one — as one as the Father and the Son are one. In His prayer, He gave three gifts to accomplish the oneness of His people: eternal life, truth (the "logos" or His Word) and His glory. When previously divided, even hostile people, can become one in this present conflicting and confusing age; then the people of the world will believe "the Father sent the Son" — our Lord Jesus Christ.

These books and their e-book compliments, as well as AUDIO on these books can be found @ www.onebody.life and on Amazon.com.